The Holy Spirit of the Bible

by

Brandon & Desiree Elrod

Ravenhill Publishing

ISBN: 978-0-98314-954-5
eISBN: 978-0-98314-953-8

LCCN: 2012910263

First Printing: 2012

Ravenhill Publishing
Santa Ana, California

Copyright © 2012 Brandon Scott Elrod www.BrandonScottElrod.com

All rights reserved, including the right of reproduction in whole or in part in any form.

Cover art by Noah www.NoahFineArt.com

Unless otherwise noted, all Scripture quotations taken from the New American Standard Bible®,
Copyright © 1960, 1962, 1963, 1968, 1971, 1972, 1973,
1975, 1977, 1995 by The Lockman Foundation
Used by permission. (www.Lockman.org)

Scripture taken from the New King James Version. Copyright © 1982 by Thomas Nelson, Inc. Used by permission. All rights reserved.

Scripture taken from the King James Version. Public Domain.

All versions accessed through Blue Letter Bible. www.BlueLetterBible.org
1996-2012 Last accessed 5/18/2012.

"I would encourage all Christians and especially those who have grown up in a fundamental church to read and react to Brandon and Desiree's book. You will be stimulated to reconsider what may be long held beliefs on the work of the Holy Spirit. By reading this book, if the Spirit of God works more fully and maturely in your life, the investment of time and thoughtful consideration of the concepts of this book will be your greatest blessing and God's greatest glory as well as build up the Church for greater service."
David Mitchell
Senior Pastor
Calvary Church of Santa Ana

"Brandon Elrod has written an important primer on the Holy Spirit, which should serve as a foundational tool to understand the transformational power of God's work in His church. There are serious misconceptions, and sadly, fears, of how the third person of the Trinity teaches and inspires believers. All too often we fail to heed the voice of the Holy Spirit and miss out on His liberating force. Therefore, we must learn that a life fully yielded to the Holy Spirit will ignite passion for God and abundant living for His glory. I commend this work to new Christians who are uncertain of the fundamentals of their faith, and to veterans who have become lukewarm and have lost the flame for God."
Al Mijares, Ph.D.
Member, Board of Trustees
Biola University

"Brandon and Desiree have sought the Lord diligently, then taken their experience of the Lord and sifted it through His Word. They present their findings in clear, genuine terms because it is their heart to share with their brothers and sisters the fullness of God they have and are discovering."
Suzan Jerome
Author, Director
Pastoral Care Ministries

"You can't read this book and ignore the Holy Spirit anymore! Brandon's background and experience will help the most conservative people recognize what it means to yield to the Holy Spirit in your life. And he writes about Him in a way that doesn't weird you out. Teaching about the Holy Spirit has been confused and manipulated over the years. This

book takes people who think of the Holy Spirit as force and power to a place of recognizing Him as God with a vital role in the life of every believer. This book takes the discussion of the Holy Spirit to a level that will challenge your thinking and open your eyes to how God works in our lives without freaking you out."
Eric Wakeling
Executive Pastor
Calvary Church of Santa Ana

"I read over 20 books each year and can truly say that "The Holy Spirit of the Bible" encouraged, enlightened, and challenged my thinking more than any other I read this year. For anyone seeking to understand and live a life of yielding to the fullness of the Holy Spirit, this is the book for you. From the first page warning that our plans often "muffle the voice of the Father" to the last page reminder that our job is simply to yield (He does all the rest), the key takeaway here is to die to oneself and find new life in the Spirit."
Rick McCarthy
Chair
Convene *Christian CEO mentoring forum*

Brandon would like to thank Mom and Dad, who laid the spiritual foundations within me and raised me to believe in a powerful and engaging God, and who furthered the heritage that our spiritual forefathers began.

Desiree would like to thank each member of her family, who God used from an early age to influence her spiritual journey, as well as her prayer group, who for the last decade has explored the possibilities and power of prayer and has experienced a deep connection with God that inspired many of the stories in this book.

Special thanks go to Suzan Jerome, Rick and Susan McCarthy, Bob Shank, El Clark and Al Mijares for their mentoring and input throughout this journey. We especially thank David Mitchell, Eric Wakeling, Jeff Biddle and Bill Shaw from our home church, Calvary Church of Santa Ana, for their investment into our ministries.

This book is dedicated to our children.
May your hearts hear the voice of God
and respond with joy
and uninhibited obedience.

Preface..11

Chapter 1
    What we are missing is the Holy Spirit............................15

Chapter 2
    A few necessary warnings about pursuing the Holy Spirit...........25

Chapter 3
    The Strategy that keeps us from the Original......................35

Chapter 4
    The Source of Authority..41

Chapter 5
    Joining the Holy Spirit..51

Chapter 6
    Essential roles of the Holy Spirit.................................63

Chapter 7
    The Seven-fold Spirit of God vs. The Seven Abominations............81

Chapter 8
    Authentic vs. counterfeit: Spiritual fruit.........................91

Chapter 9
    Authentic vs. counterfeit: Spiritual roles........................107

Chapter 10
    Authentic vs. counterfeit: Spiritual gifts........................119

Chapter 11
    Authentic vs. counterfeit: Supernatural phenomena.................141

Chapter 12
    Authentic vs. counterfeit: Superhuman ability.....................153

Chapter 13
    The creativity of the Spirit of God...............................159

Chapter 14
    The boundlessness of the Spirit of God............................167

Chapter 15
    From skeptic to believer..173

Preface

My wife, Desiree, and I believe that we all bring something unique to the table in the events of our lives: personality, strengths, gifts, passions, skills, experiences, and the sort. It is the collection of all these characteristics that comprises our core identity, the authentic person that has been predestined and preordained by the Heavenly Father.

Of course, we distort and misuse each of these characteristics when we apply our own plans and perspectives to them. Our plans and perspectives are the intangible strongholds that muffle the voice of the Father as He works to commune with us. Why are these such powerful deterrents to intimacy with Him? It is because our plans and perspectives are born out of our pride, and we know that pride is an abomination to God.

Unfortunately, when the Church speaks of "dying to self," and "crucifying the old-man," the message that is often sent is that we need to be completely replaced by something new and completely "not" who we currently are, in order for God to use us. What is the problem with this way of thinking? It assumes that God did not predestine us for a unique destiny, and much less, equip us for the task. It also makes it very difficult to know how to properly apply the principle! It is in this dark sea that many Christians flounder, unfulfilled and unused, because all of our attempts to *not* be ourselves are unsuccessful.

The reality is that God crafted each one of us for a very special role in His kingdom. "For we are His workmanship, created in Christ Jesus for *good works*, which God prepared beforehand so that we would walk in them." Ephesians 2:10 God has created good works for us to fulfill. How will we live up to this? We are told in Romans 8:29 that we have been predestined to be conformed to the image of Jesus-in other words, God is committed to shaping us into Jesus's model. What was His model? It was a lifestyle of being led by, filled by, and empowered by the Holy Spirit. God is actively involved in maturing us toward that lifestyle and those *good works*.

When we talk about being "conformed" or "putting off the old man," we are not talking about replacing our unique personality, our unique strengths, unique gifts, unique passions, unique skills and our unique experiences. Those are gifts from our Father, even if they don't make sense to us quite yet, and He expects a great return on what He has entrusted us with. What we are specifically putting to death are our *plans* and our *perspectives*.

Our plans are our priorities and agendas. Our plans are typically self-seeking, and for this reason, they must be yielded to the will of the Father. However, our plans may also seem noble from time to time, particularly when we make assumptions about what is pleasing to God. Paul and Timothy assumed that it would please God to evangelize in Asia, yet the Holy Spirit did not allow them to.[1]

Paul had noble intent; he was going to continue his ministry into Asia. How could this possibly be against the will of the Father? We don't see the immediate answer in this passage. We have to trust God, as Paul had to do when "the Spirit of Jesus" forbade him, that His grand design is trustworthy and beyond our understanding. Our perspectives are our two-dimensional presuppositions, assumptions and earned beliefs about the nature of God: what is pleasing to Him, and what He thinks of us, among other things.

When Romans states that "we are predestined to become conformed to the image of His Son," what is the "image of His Son?" It means simply this; Jesus emptied Himself of His own agenda and His perspectives so that He could fully submit Himself to the will of the Father. You may ask, naturally, "What agendas could Jesus possibly have had outside of the Father's will? Wasn't He already God, and therefore, in tune with Himself?"

Let us not forget, friends, that though Jesus was born without a sin nature, he was in all ways a human being.[2] He was tempted in every way that we are, yet without sinning. Temptation involves our fleshly desires and perspectives, and Jesus was the authoritative model on how to yield these desires, plans and perspectives. His life was spent submitting His natural desires to the desires and promptings of His Father.

If Christ was made a human being, and if we are made in His image, then we, just like Him, have been created with all the characteristics needed for the mission. All Jesus had to do to prepare was to keep "increasing in wisdom and stature, and in favor with God and men,"[3] and we are called to the same. We also, like Jesus, have to learn obedience, "Although He was a son, He learned obedience from the things which He suffered." Hebrews 5:8

---

[1] Acts 16:6-8

[2] 1 Corinthians 15:21, Hebrews 2:9, Hebrews 4:15, Romans 5:15

[3] Luke 2:52

We will look much more closely at Jesus' model to us, as He yielded Himself to the Father, in Chapter 4.

No doubt, many readers are now asking the significant question, "What about sin?" How does self-control fit into this definition of "dying to self?" In returning to the example of Jesus, we recall that He used self-control each time He was tempted. He was not mastered by sin; rather, He mastered sin. But, His life was not a pursuit of the control of sin. Jesus' control of sin was a by-product of His submission to His Father. Paul the Apostle modeled this well: He urged his readers to "Be imitators of me, just as I also am of Christ,"[4] he reminded them that "sin shall not be master over you,"[5] and confirmed his own frustrations over sin, "For the good that I want, I do not do, but I practice the very evil that I do not want."[6]

The point is this: Paul was honest about his sin, but he didn't model a pursuit of sin management. What he did model for us was a pursuit of the Father's will. Paul lived as a missionary, constantly moving from location to location, as the Spirit led. He had a regular weekly ministry in the local church. He was additionally mentoring countless people throughout his journeys, and finally, he was unwittingly writing parts of the Bible. These were his primary areas of focus and yielding; I would dare say the sin was just relegated to the status of distraction.
If God intends to employ the unique attributes He designed us with, then it is critical that we understand ourselves, His great "workmanship." It is not a selfish or egocentric exercise; rather, it is essential if we are to "grow in stature and favor." We cannot be honest with God if we cannot be honest with ourselves. We cannot be honest with ourselves if we do not *know* ourselves.

As we empty ourselves and yield to our Father, we find out that it is not the elimination of our characteristics, but rather His employment, enhancement, and empowerment of them, that He is so concerned with. Through this process of connecting with the Lover of our Souls, our gifting emerges, our passions are clarified, and our calling is revealed.

Thank you for joining us on this journey into the nature of the Holy Spirit; may you be inevitably transformed by His purpose, and may that

---

[4] 1 Corinthians 11:1

[5] Romans 6:14

[6] Romans 7:19

transformation launch you into the fulness and authority that only comes through the Spirit of God.

Chapter 1

What we are missing is the Holy Spirit

"I was living as a model of Christianity, both in study and in service. But deep inside, I had a growing sense that something was missing."

"You did not choose Me but I chose you, and appointed you that you would go and bear fruit, and that your fruit would remain, so that whatever you ask of the Father in My name He may give to you." John 15:16

It all started with the question from my young son who had just watched Star Wars. "Dad, is 'The Force' real?" For those of you who have not watched this movie or read the books, it is a fantasy story about a future struggle between good and evil throughout the galaxy. In this setting, good and evil are characterized by either "the light side" or "the dark side," both being polarized representations of "The Force," an energy that one could learn to harness and utilize. The utilization, of course, depends on your desired effect. Will you use "The Force" selflessly for the good of humanity, or will you use it selfishly to satisfy your own lust for power?

My son was quite unaware of the deeper storyline, or the world-views represented in this film, produced during an era of a great societal search for meaning, fulfillment and spirituality. Many influential Christ-followers came out of this movement, as did an influx of New Age thought and pagan belief that led into the material excess of the 1980s. My son, rather, was fascinated by the cinematic ability to use "The Force" to retrieve a light-saber without even touching it. "Dad, is 'The Force' real?" I pondered this question briefly before responding from my heart. It occurred to me that this might be a pivotal opportunity for his young heart. "Son," I replied, "There is something much, much better than 'The Force.' You think it is amazing be able to pull a weapon toward yourself by just reaching for it, or to change someone's mind by implanting thoughts in their head. What if," I asked him, "What if you could heal someone by praying for them and touching them? What if you could bring a dead person back to life?"

This was a great opportunity to impart spiritual truth to the mind of my young son, all in language that he would understand. The intent was emphatically clear in my mind. I wanted him to understand the difference between cheap parlor tricks and true miraculous happenings. You see, for every perfect gift from the Creator, for every attribute of His perfect character, for every manifestation of the great Yahweh's will, Satan has an imitation. These imitations are knock-offs, like swap-meet Rolex watches. They look like the real thing, but when tested, when examined, when scrutinized for the Maker's mark, they fail the test. As you will soon see, God's glory is the core motivation behind every authentic act of God. For this reason, we will spend substantial time in this book examining the concept of counterfeits.

Counterfeits have deliberate targets in their deceit. There are counterfeit fruits of the Spirit, gifts of the Spirit, roles of the Spirit, miracles and supernatural phenomenon. False fruits of the Spirit, for example, infiltrate the Church, appearing to be Godly, and skew people's hearts to a point that is just off target. These are the subtle ways that Satan and his fellow fallen angels, "the enemy," weasel their way into congregations and deceive people into thinking they are spiritually healthy. Counterfeit miracles, on the other hand, are much more recognizable to most Christ-followers, but I think the Church is generally afraid of them, whereas the world obsesses over these supernatural acts, ascribing glory and power to them. Just take a look at your local TV listings and see how many talk shows and primetime dramas are dedicated to the paranormal.

I personally believe that the enemy's greatest triumph in this world is in keeping the Church unaware, deceived, afraid, and naïve of its God-given role in His grand design. More specifically, I believe the enemy targets Christian men in order to keep them oblivious, disconnected, overworked, and disenfranchised, all so that they don't awaken and discover their destiny as warriors and elders for the Kingdom of God. One of the ways our enemy achieves this is by keeping us from the Heavenly Father, through any means necessary. It may be through guilt over sin, it may be through distraction and busyness, but probably and most tragically, it may be through our denial of the work of the Holy Spirit, whose primary role is to bring us to, and keep us connected with, our Father in heaven. What more effective way to cast doubt on the work of the Holy Spirit than to flat-out deny that the work even exists.

We are robbed by our fear

Our fears in life are typically born out of our instruction and experience, and the same holds true for our fears regarding the activity of the Holy Spirit.

Some of us come from settings where the Holy Spirit was simply never really spoken of. And while there was perhaps no theological slant to muddle or confuse such a person, there was also a distinct lack of models and teachers to introduce these Christians to the Spirit of God.

Others come from settings where the activity of the Holy Spirit is the main focus of teaching, preaching, evangelism and ministry in general, often outweighing teaching about Jesus or the Father. Perhaps they are taught that there are "proofs" of salvation for all believers, such as speaking in tongues. At times they may have been very uncomfortable with how the gifts of the Spirit were portrayed. Maybe they have hungered for deep intimacy with the Father, but the extremes of their church experience regarding the display of gifts only seem to scratch the surface of true spirituality.

Finally, there are those whose church background emphatically denies the miraculous activity of the Holy Spirit, particularly in the area of spiritual gifts. These people are called cessationists, as they believe that the miraculous work of the Holy Spirit ceased when the Bible finally came on the scene, or when the last apostle had died. There are differing levels of strictness in this group: some accept that God may still directly perform a rare miracle, but not through a Christian, while others do not believe in miracles at all.

I am a product of cessationist teaching-not from my parents, but from the instruction I received at Church. Cessationists are my people, and I am deeply passionate about their discovery of the heart of God as revealed by His Spirit. If you are one, I thank you genuinely for embarking on this journey with us as we safely explore the Biblical portrait of the Holy Spirit, and I would now like to pose a few questions for you to ponder. The answers to these questions may be helpful in determining whether or not you believe God still behaves the way He did throughout the Scriptures:

When was the Bible completed, therefore presumably eliminating the miraculous activity of God on earth? Was it the end of the first century A.D., by which time the books that comprise the New Testament were written in Greek, though not yet connected to the Hebrew Old Testament? Was it in the 4th century A.D., when Athanasius "organized" the collection of books that we know as the New Testament, thus formally creating a New Testament to accompany the Old Testament? Was it in the same century when Jerome translated the New Testament from Greek into Latin? Was it the end of the 14th century when John Wycliffe produced the first hand-written English bible? Was it 200 years later when the Bible officially had numbered verses added to the chapters? Was it in the 17th century when the King James Bible was printed for the masses? Was it in the 19th century when the Apocrypha was removed from Protestant bibles?

Also, who were the Apostles, and when did the last one die? Were the apostles exclusively the former disciples of Jesus? Some say that for a book to be considered for inclusion into the New Testament, the author had to be an apostle/disciple. If that is the case, then what about Mark, Luke, and Paul? These men were not part of the twelve disciples. If we accept others' definition of an apostle, it would have to be someone who saw Jesus firsthand. But what about Barnabas, Timothy, Silvanus, Priscilla and Aquila, whom many consider to be apostles? What is the definition of an apostle? In the Greek, apostolos means: a delegate, messenger, one sent forth with orders. The Bible uses the term apostle in two contexts, the narrow sense of the twelve (minus Judas plus Paul), and in the broader sense of someone advancing the kingdom of God and employing signs and miracles. Have there truly been no apostles since 95 AD?

What is the point of all this? It is this; at what point in history did the written word become more significant than the actual work of the Spirit of God? How do you define when the complete Bible presented itself to humanity? At what point in history did the Bible become "perfection?" As a bred cessationist, we use the following scripture to illustrate the Bible's perfection and superiority over the actual gifts, miracles, and divine works of God that it speaks of.

"But when the perfect comes, the partial will be done away. When I was a child, I used to speak like a child, think like a child, reason like a child; when I became a man, I did away with childish things. For now we see in a mirror dimly, but then face to face; now I know in part, but then I will know fully just as I also have been fully known." 1 Corinthians 13:10-12

The "perfect" is the Bible, and the "partial" is the supernatural working of the Holy Spirit, according to a cessationist's explanation. I don't know about you, but when I stop to consider the gravity of this statement, it suddenly seems so backward. Apparently, now that the Bible is here, you and I engage face to face with God, like Moses on Mount Sinai. Remember the glow that he came back with after his encounter with the great Jehovah? Also, you and I supposedly know God fully, just as He knows us. And, we do so exclusively by reading the Bible. Does this represent the Christianity that you live? Does it represent my experience of God? This is obviously not the case, is it?

In other words, God is perfect, but the Holy Spirit is not, and that is why He was just a temporary solution until He could send His children *paper*. Really?

This well known scripture is actually embedded in perhaps the most famous chapter in the Bible. 1 Corinthians 13 is the "love" chapter, illustrating the superiority and authority of love as the Holy Spirit enables it. It details how love is the necessary ingredient for our spirituality to not reek of ineffectiveness and annoyance. In this context, love, and therefore, the Father Himself, as He is LOVE,[7] is that which is perfect. If God is that which is perfect, how can the Holy Spirit then be considered only partial? When will all these things converge: seeing Him face to face, knowing Him fully, and the end of love's bearing, believing, hoping and enduring all things? I have no other choice now than to believe it is when we die and enter His presence, forever to be in constant communion with Him, unfettered and uninhibited.

As a final note on the matter before moving on, let us not forget the admonition that Jesus gave the Pharisees regarding their perspective of the Scriptures:

"You search the Scriptures because you think that in them you have eternal life; it is these that testify about Me; and you are unwilling to come to Me so that you may have life." John 5:39, 40

My friends, and fellow students of the Scriptures, we do not want to be focused on the creation over the Creator. We do not want to "miss the forest for the trees." We will ultimately be miserable if we focus our pursuit on Bible knowledge alone and fail to pursue the Heavenly Father of the Bible Himself. We must remember that the Bible is the roadmap to Jesus Christ, and therefore, to the Father through the conduit of the Holy Spirit. Life in the Spirit is a life that experiences the function and the inspiration of God firsthand.

This is essential-not only to serve as an outward witness of God for unbelievers, but at a more elementary level, to provide evidence within ourselves of the marvelous and miraculous work of God for our own rooting and growth in the faith. As a result, there will be outward fruit, and it will be authoritative and powerful, because it was born out of a genuine, inward work of the Holy Spirit.

The Need for Experience

So, what can happen if we do not experience the work of the Spirit of God for ourselves? Biblically, the evidence shows a rapid "falling away"

---

[7] 1 John 4:8

of God's people. Let us look at the example set by three generations of the children of Israel after the Exodus from Egypt:

Generation 1-Deuteronomy 29:1-9
The first generation was the people that saw God do supernatural things through Moses. God brought about the plagues, they crossed the Red Sea, and He gave them water out of the rock and manna from the sky. God physically descended in a pillar of smoke by day and fire by night to lead them to the Promised Land.

Generation 2-Judges 2:7
The second generation heard the amazing stories from their parents, and they went on to win some battles with the Lord's help. They faithfully recounted the stories to their children and they served the LORD all the days of Joshua and his administration.

Generation 3-Judges 2:10-12
The third generation, however, is where everything broke down. These are the grandchildren of the people that experienced God in supernatural ways. They heard all the stories of God's power and deliverance, but they did not experience it for themselves, nor did they see great evidence of it in the lives of their parents. They were living off of the faith of their grandparents. They ultimately filled this need for experience by pursuing the counterfeits, the gods of the heathen. Stories of Jehovah had become just that-stories, legends, and lore.

There is an old proverb that states, "What I hear, I forget; what I see, I remember, what I do, I understand." As a general rule, this applies to Christianity! It applied to the 3 generations from Judges, and it still applies today! When we only *hear* about what God has done in the world, we quickly forget about Him and the reality and tangibility of His Kingdom here on earth. When we simply *observe* God at work outside of our personal sphere, we remember the observances, but they do not typically transform us. However, when we yield ourselves to God and *He empowers and works through us*, we start to understand, to the extent our human faculties allow, the heart of God and the working of the Holy Spirit. God becomes very real to us at that point.

Let's fast forward to Jesus' death, burial and resurrection. He left us the Holy Spirit. Why? In the Old Testament, priests, kings and prophets were primarily the people who were anointed in the Holy Spirit. They were the ones that God did supernatural things through. While none of us are actual kings these days, we today are priests, prophets, and other roles that He instituted. "But you are A CHOSEN RACE, A royal PRIESTHOOD, A HOLY NATION, A PEOPLE FOR God's OWN POSSESSION, so that you may proclaim the excellencies of Him who has called you out of darkness into His marvelous light; for you once were NOT A PEOPLE, but now you are THE PEOPLE OF GOD..." 1 Peter 2:9, 10a

It is critical for God's people, His royal priests, His adopted sons and daughters, to experience Him directly, just as the first generation did in the model from the children of Israel. The good news is that He gave us the Holy Spirit in order to facilitate this experience.[8] Why? Is it for the establishment of the Church? Is it for the furtherance of the Gospel? How about this; we must experience God in a supernatural way so that we do not fall away, so our faith does not become relegated to the status of fable, and so the generation behind us does not become apostate. Knowing God and knowing *about* God are two entirely different things. Knowing *about* God is the result of instruction, while *knowing* God is a result of walking in the spirit: hearing His voice and responding, and continually checking in with the Father in order to be led, inspired, confirmed, challenged, invited, and all the other actions that He uses to draw us into communion with him. Knowing *about* God is critical-it is the foundational teaching that Hebrews 6 refers to. *Knowing* God is even more critical-it is precisely what Jesus calls *eternal life* in John 17:3.

Our personal relationship with God is granted by having faith in Jesus Christ and the redemption He made possible by dying on the cross and rising from the dead. That relationship is then developed by the Spirit of God interacting within us on the Father's behalf. If Jesus Christ is the bridge, the mediator, between God and man, then we might accurately describe the Holy Spirit as the "Crossing Guard" that ushers us initially and leads us continually into fellowship and fullness in the Father.

At the point of salvation, two things occur. The first is that we believe with our hearts and confess with our mouths that Jesus is Lord.[9] The second is that our spirits are brought to life by the Holy Spirit.[10] In other words, we are connected with the Father by both external and internal proofs. We consciously and genuinely proclaim that Jesus is Lord. We follow this by being baptized. These are the outward evidences of conversion. The Church places a lot of emphasis on these things, and for good reason; they come straight out of Scripture. However, the second evidence is so often overlooked. Our spirit is brought to life by His Spirit! This is nothing short of a miracle occurring within us! Your spirit, through the Holy Spirit,

---

[8] Romans 5:5 Hebrews 6:4,5 Ephesians 1:3

[9] Romans 10:9

[10] Romans 8:10,11

now has unrestricted access to the King of Kings! This changes everything!

Yet, it is here that we can identify the subtle strategy of the enemy to keep us disengaged and estranged from our Father. Jesus told us, "You must be born of water and the Spirit" John 3:6. This is the core of our salvation and new life with our Father, and our enemy works to keep us unaware of this connection, or fearful of it. In our fear, or perhaps ignorance, Christians focus on the external proofs of the faith. We pursue knowing about God (mind) instead of knowing God (spirit). Many of us completely ignore this essential connection with our spirit and His, while others are led astray by faulty teaching. We must grow in our understanding of the Holy Spirit if we are to fully grow as children of God. Likewise, the Church, the Bride of Christ, must grow in its understanding of the Holy Spirit if it is to fully prepare for her Bridegroom.

Samuel Chadwick, writing 75 years ago, describes the bane of institutionalized religion:

> "...the one essential equipment of the Church is the gift of the Holy Ghost. Nothing else avails for the real work of the Church...Apart from Him wisdom becomes folly, and strength weakness. Scholarship is blind to spiritual truth till he reveals. Worship is idolatry till He inspires. Preaching is powerless if it be not a demonstration of His power. Prayer is vain unless He energize. Human resources of learning and organization, wealth and enthusiasm, reform and philanthropy, are worse than useless if there be no Holy Ghost in them. The Church always fails at the point of self-confidence. When the Church is run on the same lines as a circus, there may be crowds, but there is no Shekinah...Miracles are the direct work of His power, and without miracles the Church cannot live...Education can civilize, but it is being born of the Spirit that saves."[11]

I come from a well-established family in a popular, knowledge based, and Bible-centric church. I was a "good son" in the sense that I carried the torch. I was involved in ministry at many levels, and over many years. I taught about the Bible, I led missions trips; I led "worship services." And yet, through all my getting of knowledge, I felt lacking in some capacity. I attributed it to a lack of spirituality. So, I did what any good Christian does, I joined an "accountability group," a small group of people committed to vulnerability, sharing each other's struggles and encouraging each other on to good works. I remember the moment clearly-it was a defining moment in my faith. I had become so focused,

---

[11] "The Way to Pentecost," by Samuel Chadwick

so diligent to become more faithful in my "quiet times," that I had finally reached the pinnacle of Christian life; I was consistently reading the Bible, every day of the week. I even read the Bible on Sundays, outside of Church! I remember that my group mates were really happy for me, and essentially dismissed me from any of the "sin management" questions normally asked, as I clearly had reached a spiritual plane that freed me from the trappings of temptation and sin. I was bewildered at the experience. You see, in my robotic regularity, I was only going through the motions. Sure, I tried to muster some appreciation for the process, but I distinctly remember feeling disappointed that my performance had not yielded the intimacy that I expected. It was in this moment that I remember being honest with God for the first time. I admitted, however fearfully, to the God of the universe, that I felt dead inside, despite all the time I had spent with Him. I admitted to Him that I was not getting anything out of the all the dutiful "quiet times," and I was pretty sure that He wasn't getting anything out of it either. It was so dry and lifeless. I came to a powerful conclusion that would usher me into a new phase in my development in the Spirit. I concluded that the Christianity I knew, my Christianity, was not, could not possibly be, the same Christianity that people had been martyred for throughout the centuries. My Christianity could not be what had propelled the faith through all the oppression God's people suffered through persecution.

So, not knowing what else to do, I gave God an ultimatum. I know, it sounds sacrilegious. I told God that I was going to stop. I was going to stop the reading. I was going to stop the praying. I was going to stop accountability. I was going to stop ministering; oh God Almighty, was I certainly going to stop ministering. What in the world was I perpetuating in other people? I told Him I was going to stop everything, and just wait for Him to do something. I told Him that I was out of ideas, that I had tried everything and that nothing was working. I told Him that He would have to do something to make my faith real. I expected Him to.

After the first year passed, I started to get concerned. I was still going to Church, I was still present, but He wasn't doing anything. I remember starting to question my salvation. I went to the Bible for reassurance, and I came up with three measurables that I thought would be sufficient enough to confirm my salvation. If I was truly saved, then I should exhibit the following characteristics: I should experience the conviction of the Holy Spirit, I should exhibit the fruits of the Spirit, and I should have power over demons.

Well, needless to say, I was quickly disappointed. I realized that I couldn't effectively distinguish the voice of the Holy Spirit from my own moral conscience! I had been raised with all the rules, so I knew all the right answers in my head. Moving on to the fruits of the Spirit, "love, joy, peace, etc." didn't help either. "What if I am naturally a peacemaker?" I wondered. Finally, I knew that I had experienced power over the enemy. But, again, no help, as Jesus Himself told people that had cast out demons to depart from Him, as He did not know them.[12]

I remember experiencing a little panic. I met up with a dear friend of mine, and I asked him directly, "How do you know that you are saved!?" I will never forget his answer. "Oh, that's easy; my spirit communes with His Spirit!" I nodded my head in agreement and smiled, but I had no idea as to what he was talking about. I knew him well; we had the same conservative background, so I knew I could trust him as a reliable source. He went on to describe to me what he meant. He was talking about the need to engage with the Holy Spirit. He was talking about abiding-being sensitive to the promptings, the invitations, and the leading of the Spirit of God. He was talking about hearing from God.

Why do we rarely hear about the activity of the Holy Spirit in conservative churches? Well, it is quite simple. If you do not believe that His role is viable anymore, as in the dissolution of gifts and miracles, then what is left to expound upon? He becomes nothing more than a "comforting force" or a "unifying vibe" when believers come together. He gets relegated to the role of "silent prayer partner" as we imagine Romans 8:26 to mean.

You see, I had so much knowledge about God and so much practical training, my spiritual resume looked pretty good on paper. But, it was all blah. My "spiritual" words were nothing more than regurgitated rhetoric. There was no life in them. There was no power and no authority. There was no compassion. There was no mercy. There was no love. There was no evidence of the Spirit of God behind and through all my vain words and actions! There was none because I was the power source and the motivation, not God. I was the clanging cymbal from 1 Corinthians 13!

Ladies and gentlemen, we invite you to join fellow evangelical Christians, rooted in knowledge, students of the Scriptures, to explore the role of the Holy Spirit throughout the Bible. We invite you to take a journey with us in celebration of an oft-neglected member of the Trinity, in an examination of His role throughout human history. We hope you finish this book amazed and excited about the Holy Spirit. More so, we pray that your heart will be open to hearing His voice and growing in intimacy with our Heavenly Father.

---

[12] Matthew 7:21

Chapter 2

A Few Necessary Warnings About Pursuing the Holy Spirit

"I knew so much about God, but I did not know Him."

If you, as a follower of Jesus Christ, are reading this book and you relate with the descriptors, "oblivious, disconnected, overworked, and disenfranchised," and you are at a point of knowing something has to change, you are not alone. The journey for so many of us is one of a foundationally solid, yet academic Christianity that ultimately reaches a T-intersection. We thought the road we were on was a straight line to eternity itself, yet we reached a point of deadness that couldn't be remedied by adding more Bible or finding more ways to serve. We are at a crossroads in our faith; we must choose what direction we will go. The road to the left leads away from faith. Have you just had enough with the institutional answer for spirituality? Are you ready to walk away from it all out of frustration with what you have experienced (or not) so far?

The road behind you is safe; it is the path of duty. You know exactly the ground it follows. There will be little risk if you decide to play it safe and go with a known equation. You also know that there will be little hope for fulfillment, but you've met lots of folks that live their entire existence on this road, roaming the entire length of it, back and forth. Some of them are inspirational in their own right: they read the Bible, a lot, they know a lot of Scripture, and they model a picture perfect existence to those on the outside. Many of them even have positions of leadership and respect. You find yourself weighing the options.

Yet, still, the road to the right beckons. It is the road to fullness. You don't know why exactly, but this road produces an anxiety and a longing all at once. You try to look down the road for clues as to the level of risk you would be taking, but it yields no hints. You are still perplexed that the road you've come down doesn't go straight through! Do you take the risk? Do you engage with the emotions that this road seems to elicit?

You retrace your journey in your mind, and arrive back at this crux. You have been in accountability groups, you have served your church in every capacity imaginable, you have had consistent "quiet times" recently in a final attempt to push through the deadness, and it all led you here. Your logic tells you that to retrace these steps would only lead you back to the same frustrating conclusion, "My Christianity cannot be the same Christianity that people have been martyred for." You have tried everything you can think of, and you are out of options. With the sort of resolve that only desperation knows, you decide upon the road to the right.

Warning One-the Pursuit of Experience

As Christians set off down the road of discovery in the spiritual realm, it is critical that we present the need for caution. You see, it is the desire of the wicked one, the enemy of our souls, to thwart and distract us in general, but even more so on our road to experiencing God and discovering His destiny for us. Satan will use anything from the obvious to the subtle, but most often, the subtle, to keep us from fullness in Christ. As we begin to experience the working of the Holy Spirit in our hearts, the enemy will try to rob us and taint the experience.

A very common way he does this is to take our gaze off of the Heavenly Father, our Father of Lights (James 1:17), from whom every good and perfect gift flows, and tempt us to be focused on the experience itself. You don't have to look very far to find this happening. When you talk with people that are "Spirit-filled," is their focus on being with their Heavenly Father, or is it on replicating an experience? Is there some need or compulsion to "get back" to a feeling or a manifestation of the Holy Spirit, or to return to their First Love?

There is a tendency for people, once they experience a moving of the Holy Spirit, to chase that experience relentlessly. "How is that wrong?" you may ask. Here is the reason: it is wrong to pursue a manifestation in place of God Himself, because it is wrong to pursue the created thing in place of the Creator. Why do we do this? We do it because it is tangible, and we desperately want a solid representation of God that we can stick in the bank; it is guaranteed, it is not blind faith, it is not speculation, it is not one of many belief systems. It is right and true because we have physical proof. This is the problem the children of Israel had. They grew weary of following God in the cloud and in the fire. They wanted a physical representation they could relate with. They wanted God on their terms, so God gave them judges and kings. He gave them authority and truth in human form. He accommodated their grumblings. Sometimes, that wasn't even enough.

Out of the book of Judges, we see an example of this human blight, this need for tangibility. "Now there was a man of the hill country of Ephraim whose name was Micah. He said to his mother, "The eleven hundred pieces of silver which were taken from you, about which you uttered a curse in my hearing, behold, the silver is with me; I took it." And his mother said, "Blessed be my son by the LORD." He then returned the eleven hundred pieces of silver to his mother, and his mother said, "I wholly dedicate the silver from my hand to the LORD for my son to make a graven image and a molten image; now therefore, I will return them to you." So when he returned the silver to his mother, his mother took two hundred pieces of silver and gave them to the silversmith who made them into a graven image and a molten image, and they were in the house of Micah. And the man Micah had a shrine and he made an ephod and household idols and consecrated one of his sons that he might become his priest. In those days there was no king in Israel; every man did what was right in his own eyes." Judges 17:1-6

This man, Micah, made idols to Yahweh. He made a shrine to Yahweh. His family now had a representation of Jehovah they could touch and put their hope in.

Jesus later addressed a similar issue with the Pharisees, religious leaders who put great stock in their duty and rule-keeping. They took great pride in being noticed when they fasted, or when they wanted to be perceived as fasting. They were students of the law and the prophets, as Paul later describes. Jesus says to these men in John 5:39-40, "You search the Scriptures because you think that in them you have eternal life; it is these that testify about Me; and you are unwilling to come to Me so that you may have life." This is such a poignant verse; we will revisit it again and again. Jesus calls the Pharisees on the carpet for knowing the Scriptures inside and out, yet completely missing the message of them.

Warning Two-the Pursuit of Power

Our second warning speaks to the tendency of some to crave the power that comes from the Spirit. It is a sobering thing to experience the power of God in a personal way. If a person is in community with other believers who experience God in similar ways, there is a built-in system of "checks and balances" to keep the Body balanced. For this reason, God instructs us to "Let two or three prophets speak, and let the others pass judgment. But if a revelation is made to another who is seated, the first one must keep silent. For you can all prophesy one by one, so that all may learn and all may be exhorted; and the spirits of prophets are subject to prophets; for God is not a God of confusion but of peace, as in all the churches of the saints." 1 Corinthians 14:29-33

However, where a person is not in such a community, there is the human potential to elevate and honor this person in a way that creates pride. Such a person is in danger of pursuing the power of the Spirit for the glory of men. Acts 8:9-24 illustrates the danger of the pursuit of power, respect, experience, gain and the sort, when it comes to the working of the Holy Spirit. There was a man named Simon (not Peter) who saw the miraculous work that Philip was doing, and how the people were beginning to believe in the name of Jesus as a result. He also professed faith and followed Philip around for a while. Now, even though the people had professed faith in Jesus, they had not yet received the Holy Spirit, so Peter and John came down and began laying hands on the new believers, and the people began receiving the Holy Spirit.

"Now when Simon saw that the Spirit was bestowed through the laying on of the apostles' hands, he offered them money, saying, "Give this authority to me as well, so that everyone on whom I lay my hands may receive the Holy Spirit." But Peter said to him, "May your silver perish with you, because you thought you could obtain the gift of God with money! "You have no part or portion in this matter, for your heart is not right before God. "Therefore repent of this wickedness of yours, and pray the Lord that, if possible, the intention of your heart may be forgiven you. "For I see that you are in the gall of bitterness and in the bondage of iniquity." But Simon answered and said, "Pray to the Lord for me yourselves, so that nothing of what you have said may come upon me."

This man, Simon, desired the power of the Holy Spirit for completely selfish reasons; He wanted the power. And, one thing will become increasingly clear as we continue our journey together, the Holy Spirit shares the spotlight with no one. And, in a trademark of a balanced church body, his fellow Christians called him on the carpet for his folly.

Warning Three-the Pursuit of Selfish Agendas

Charles Finney wrote on this very topic, addressing the reasons why we Christians too often do not receive the filling of the Holy Spirit:

"Often your motive in asking for the Spirit is merely personal comfort and consolation--as if you would live all your spiritual life on sweet-meats. Others ask for it really as a matter of self-glorification. They would like to have their names emblazoned in the papers. It would be so gratifying to be held up as a miracle of grace--as a most remarkable Christian. Alas, how many in various forms of it, are only offering selfish prayers!

It is common for persons to resist the Spirit in the very steps He chooses to take. They would make the Spirit yield to them; He would have them yield to Him. They think only of having their blessings come in the way of their own choosing; He is wiser and will do it in His own way or not at all. If they cannot accept of His way, there can be no agreement. Often when persons pray for the Spirit, they have in their minds certain things which they would dictate to Him as to the manner and circumstances. Such ought to know that if they would have the Spirit, they must accept Him in

His own way. Let Him lead, and consider that your business is to follow. Thus it not infrequently happens that professed Christians maintain a perpetual resistance against the Holy Spirit, even while they are ostensibly praying for His presence and power. When He would fain draw them, they are thinking of dictating to Him, and refuse to be led by Him in His way. When they come really to understand what is implied in being filled with the Spirit, they draw back. It is more and different from what they had thought. That is not what they wanted."[13]

A few years ago, Desiree attended a conference to learn more about the work of the Holy Spirit. A couple approached her after learning of Desiree's gifting, and wanted her to lay hands on them so they too could gain her spiritual gifting. It seemed that they were trying to catalog and amass as many spiritual gifts as they could, especially gifts that appeared more significant than others. This experience was unnerving for Desiree, to say the least, and it was clear that this was not pleasing to God. Selfish agendas were fueling this "pursuit" of the Holy Spirit.

In case you are wanting to use Romans 1:11 to justify the idea of transferring a spiritual gift to another person, you must understand the passage clearly. "For I long to be with you, that I may impart to you some spiritual gift, and that you and I may mutually build each other up in the faith." The word "impart" here means "share" as distinguished from the word "give." Paul is looking forward to sharing, and therefore, ministering to his fellow saints.

Let us not be unaware, of course, of our own flesh and its ambitions. Yes, the enemy does tempt and distract in this area, but the reality is that our own selfish desires need to checked and confessed to the Father. The Bible lays out some very elementary instructions as to the use of the gifts of the Spirit, because some people in the early church were incorrectly elevating the status of some gifts, and others were misusing the gifts; they were operating in the flesh instead of aligning with the authentic work of the Holy Spirit. It was no different then as it is today in that regard.

Warning Four-the Possibility of Regression

"For in the case of those who have once been enlightened and have tasted of the heavenly gift and have been made partakers of the Holy Spirit, and have tasted the good word of God and the powers of the age

---

[13] "The Oberlin Evangelist: On Prayer for the Holy Spirit," May 23, 1855 Charles Finney

to come, and then have fallen away, it is impossible to renew them again to repentance, since they again crucify to themselves the Son of God and put Him to open shame." Hebrews 6:4-6

In the context of our discussion, this passage presents a stern Biblical warning. It is possible for a mature Christian to fall away. It is possible for a person to walk and talk with God and still fall to temptation. We must maintain this realistic understanding of our human nature and not deceive ourselves into thinking that we are "above" certain behaviors and motivations. This was true for Adam, Abraham, and the Apostle Peter. A quick look at the life of Moses will illustrate this perfectly.

In Numbers 20, Moses is told by God to speak to the rock and water would flow forth for the children of Israel. Moses instead snaps at the people with a verbal jab and strikes the rock. God still performs a miracle and provides water, but Moses is reprimanded by God for being irreverent, and the punishment is that he cannot enter the Promised Land. Is it possible that the same happens today? Is it possible that works of power, healing and miracles still happen, yet not in compliance with the heart of God?

Here's an example from the life of Peter. Peter has a great vision from God-do you remember it? In this vision, God shows Peter a blanket, lowering from the sky, and it contains different kinds of unclean animals. A voice tells Peter to kill and eat the animals. Of course, Peter refuses because the animals were unclean. But, God responds by telling him that He had now made them clean. This vision was Peter's official call by God to minister to the Gentiles. Peter obeys and miraculous events follow.

However, just a short time after, we see that Peter is behaving in fear and is dishonoring what God had just proven to him. We pick up the story in Galatians 2:11, "But when Peter came to Antioch, I (Paul) opposed him to his face, because he stood condemned. For prior to the coming of certain men from James, he used to eat with the Gentiles; but when they came, he began to withdraw and hold himself aloof, fearing the party of the circumcision. The rest of the Jews joined him in hypocrisy, with the result that even Barnabas was carried away by their hypocrisy."

Peter essentially reverts back to his mindset before the great vision, before the miracles, and he once again treats the Gentiles like they are unclean. He plays the hypocrite out of fear of the Jewish Christians in attendance. I am positive this was not premeditated. I am sure that Peter just got caught up in his own insecurities, but in doing so, he quickly regressed to a place of being in opposition to the work of the Holy Spirit.

Warning Five: the Danger of Labels

Why are we so obsessed with categorizing and naming things? Is it an inherent need for organization? Probably not. I believe that we humans are so desirous of formulas, that we have to chronicle, tabulate and label even the spiritual aspects of life. We love formulas because it is easier to persuade someone when we can present an encapsulated, nicely packaged, concept. We love formulas because they tell us exactly how much (or little) we have to do to get by. Finally, we love formulas because we take pride in being part of movements. Aligning with a movement is our way feeling "right" and "correct," even if our movement is an anti-movement.

The trouble with Church movements is that they never stay movements. Movements are typically driven by the passion and calling of a few, and many are swept up into them. This is about the time that movements have to start labeling things and creating positions. As a movement begins to be run by converts, it transitions into something else entirely. This second wave of members oftentimes consists of people that have become polarized and loyal to the cause, rather than to the complete representation of a God who is beyond understanding. Great examples of this are the Calvinist and Arminianist camps. Calvinists focus on God's sovereignty and predestination, while Arminianists focus on mankind's responsibility and free will. Both sides, ever since they first gained their labels, have debated the issues and have questioned each other's intent and integrity. The truth is that we cannot stamp our labels on God, for as soon as we stamp Him as Love, we will minimize His justice. As soon as we label Him as omnipotent, we forget His tenderness. And as soon as we stamp Him as the Lamb, we cheapen His role as the Lion.

Reality is that God defies labels, because He cannot be contained by our best explanation of His attributes. He is the God of Calvinism, and He most certainly is the God of Arminianism. He is altogether both, whether we understand how it is possible or not. So then, what do we need these labels for if they serve to cause division and fail to completely describe the indescribable God?

I would assert that we need labels in order to understand theology; after all, the word "Trinity" is a label. It is not a word that is found in the Bible, yet it is foundational to our understanding of our faith. Labels are helpful for building the foundations of our spiritual childhood and adolescence. As we move into spiritual fatherhood and motherhood, however, grasping at labels begins to be an entrapment and a distraction.

When my father asked evangelist Leonard Ravenhill, near the end of his life, whether he was a Calvinist or an Arminianist, the response was memorable. He looked at my father with a quizzical, yet unaffected look. "What in the world does that have to do with anything?" his silence seemed to indicate. He was almost perturbed at the inquiry. He was a man that was always, only, about his Father's business.

As A.W. Tozer writes in "Whatever Happened to Worship," "That is why I cannot get all heated up about contending for one theological side or another on that issue. If Isaac Watts, a Calvinist, could write such praise to God and John Wesley, an Arminian, could sing it with yearning and they both can meet and hug one another in glory, why should I allow anyone to force me to confess, "I don't know which I am!" Why should anyone bother me with an issue like that?"

There is no question, friends, that the Spirit of God is at work in our time. We see amazing works of God on a regular basis, and the temptation is to try to wrap our arms around it and make it ours. Unfortunately, that is the quickest way to quench the Spirit and resume, inadvertently, in a counterfeit of His authentic work. To this end, brothers and sisters, we renounce the labels that people want to ascribe to current events in the Church. We are not part of any movement; there is nothing "new" happening here to stamp a name onto. Instead, God is still about His business as He always has been, and praise be to His holy name for inviting us to join Him in His work.

Warning Six: Ramifications

We have biographies upon biographies of people that lived in alignment with the heart of God and dependence on His voice. These people have become "pillars of the faith" and we love to quote their sayings. Have you ever noticed that a consistent similarity between most of these people is that they stood out uncomfortably in their faith and devotion to God?

One of our highest hurdles is the difficulty we have in departing the traditions of men. We often substitute denominational beliefs and requirements for the simplicity of God, so letting go of them can be an intensive process, even with the Holy Spirit "propelling" us in our epiphanies. It is so difficult for Evangelical Christians to stand out uncomfortably because the system has been designed to be the final authority on the nature of God. We, more than any other Christian group, "know" we are correct. Why? It is because we are Evangelicals, and by nature, we hold to the highest Biblical standards and judge the rest of Christendom and the world by them. As a result, we find great safety in hiding in theology, because, even though we may be desolate and disillusioned in our experience (or lack of) with God, at least we are "correct." What great despair; what great doom, to believe that our proper tradition is correct, yet to be completely unfulfilled in it.

When the Father starts to illuminate the darkness in our hearts, the recesses, and invite us into surrender and communion with Him, we start to stand out uncomfortably. We start using words like yielding and releasing, and listening and abiding, words that tend to invoke quizzical looks from other believers.

To side with God and move with Him means that we will sever certain cords in the world of traditions which have imposed limitations on the Spirit of God. We must be prepared for this, especially since it is the compelling influence of the approval of man, "fitting in" to an environment that represents the ultimate authority on the nature of God, that keeps us and God in a box. However, and inevitably, the genuine evidence of the Holy Spirit is irresistible! People will ultimately be drawn to Him through you. A difference in your own spirit will be noticeable, and it will sweetly reflect the nature of God to those around you. People will notice in you what they have been missing out on in their own relationship with God, and He will be glorified as you minister to them.

Jesus said, "You search the Scriptures because you think that in them you have eternal life; it is these that testify about Me; and you are unwilling to come to Me so that you may have life." John 5:39, 40

We must be very, very careful to not be so rigid in our assumptions about God that we completely miss the creative ways He works.

No doubt, you, the scholarly student of Scripture and dedicated Evangelical, are reading a subversive message between the lines here. Please do not misunderstand what we are saying! The Evangelical Church is wary and cautious-those are wonderful traits! We are exhorted in Scripture to be wary. The Church is the Bride of Christ, eagerly awaiting her bridegroom, and in no way do we intend any disservice to His great design. It is not about *reinventing* Christianity-rather it is about *rediscovering* it! There is nothing wrong with Christianity. We do not desire to make it more appealing to the world. We simply want to release Christians to learn to abide in Christ, to live in the Spirit, to commune with the Father. Evangelical teaching lays a solid foundation to build on; and the truth of Scripture is absolutely essential as we begin to grow into maturity as believers.

Chapter 3

The Strategy that Keeps Us from the Original

"The more I got to know the Father, the less I feared the gimmicks of the enemy."

Let us not be deceived in our comparison of the supernatural, of truth versus lies. Jesus said, "I am the way, I am the truth, and I am the life. No man comes to the Father except through me."[14] Jesus is the Word and He is the Truth. Satan is the Lie. "Whenever he speaks a lie, he speaks from his own nature, for he is a liar and the father of lies."[15]

God is the Original and the Source; He created everything. Not only does this include organic and inorganic beings and entities, nature, and light, but He also created theory and principle and inspiration, as well as all the other innumerable and intangible aspects of life. That, of course, means that He created heaven and hell. He created hell as a place of punishment for the angels that chose to rebel against Him. God is the Originator. He is the Architect, the Engineer, and the Artist.

On the flip-side, Satan is the pretender; He is the fabrication, both as a created being and as a product of his own pride. He thought more highly of himself than he should, and devised a plan to take over heaven. And, as darkness cannot hide in the light, his plan was exposed and he was seen for the charlatan he made himself to be, and God dealt swiftly with this created being who thought he could "get a piece of the action." Isaiah 14 describes how Satan fell from heaven because he intended to exalt his own throne to be like God.

Let us be crystal clear; we are not caught in a cosmic tug-of-war between God and Satan. God is the original and Satan is a created being. "For by Him all things were created, both in the heavens and on earth, visible and invisible, whether thrones or dominions or rulers or authorities--all things have been created through Him and for Him."[16]

Satan is only a fallen angel. He is not a deity. God is not struggling against Satan. There is absolutely an unseen war, but it is not a struggle; the victory is God's.

---

[14] John 14:6

[15] John 8:44

[16] Colossians 1:16

Stigmatization of the Unseen

In our Western culture, we are skeptical of the spiritual realm: the *unseen* realm, and quite honestly, we are skeptical of any person that claims to have encountered it. The Church has also sold its collective soul to post-modern rationalism and science's empirical measure. Since we cannot chart, graph and quantify the spiritual realm, we really don't take seriously the activity of demons and angels. For those in the Church that do, however, there is often a disproportionate perspective that leads to fear of the spiritual realm.

Blame it on Hollywood if you want, with their sensationalizing of demons and the occult. Whatever the reason, when Christians have a disproportionate view of the spiritual realm, they tend to minimize the significance of the role of angels, and magnify the role of demons and anything under their purview. The reality of the heavenly realm is that there are several types of angels with different ranks and functions. When angels appear in *human* form in the Scriptures, people are generally unaware of their true form, and as such, interact with them as though they were human. However, when angels manifest in their true supernatural form, people are typically quite frightened.

"And an angel of the Lord appeared to him, standing to the right of the altar of incense. Zacharias was troubled when he saw the angel, and fear gripped him. But the angel said to him, "Do not be afraid, Zacharias, for your petition has been heard, and your wife Elizabeth will bear you a son, and you will give him the name John."[17]

Zacharias was afraid before the angel. Of course he was. John fell to his knees before an angel but was met with refusal. "Then I fell at his feet to worship him. But he said to me, "Do not do that; I am a fellow servant of yours and your brethren who hold the testimony of Jesus; worship God. For the testimony of Jesus is the spirit of prophecy."[18]

It is natural to have a fear of the unseen. It is nearly impossible for our minds to compute the possibilities of the supernatural realm. Our intellect is beholden to the restraints of physics. The supernatural is not. We tend to fear the enemy even more so, because the enemy is determined to

---

[17] Luke 1:11-13

[18] Revelation 19:10

thwart and distract us. We have an unseen enemy that has an unfair advantage in oppressing us. It doesn't seem like a fair fight. It isn't.

I don't mean that it isn't fair *against* us; quite the opposite! We are the victors! It isn't a fair fight because *we* have the advantage! "What in the world are you talking about?" you may be asking. Let me tell you all the ways the battle is lopsided in our favor. We have already been guaranteed the victory, and beyond strength in numbers, we also have the Holy Spirit working behind the scenes to unify and strengthen the children of God. Angelic beings long to understand what the experience of salvation and grace is like,[19] as we have the privilege of being given this great gift exclusively. Why humans? Why is salvation not for sinful angels as well? I don't know. We both have sinned. We have both fallen. Humans are incorrigible, ungrateful and rebellious. Why are we extended this grace? Additionally, we have greater numbers. The Bible indicates that the fallen angels constitute a minority of the total number: Engaged Christ-followers + angels + God=The Lord's Army. And finally, our Commander is Jesus Himself;[20] He is not a bureaucrat-He is a fighter.[21]

Satan's Tactics

Satan is *the* lie. He is the father of lies. What is the logical tactic of a defeated rebel? Do as much damage as possible on the way out. Spread as many lies as possible before incarceration. We see plainly how he works in the world, but do we recognize how he works in the Church? He spreads lies, but in order to fly under the radar, his lies are subtle and are directed at our wounds. He strikes with precision, and unless we are carrying the shield of faith, it is difficult to deflect the fiery darts.

We will iterate and reiterate throughout this book that Satan's greatest influence will be in neutering the warriors of the Kingdom. How? With lies that undermine our authority in the Lord, and the fear and doubt that come with them. Authority is an easy target, because if you've never experienced it, you don't know what it looks like. It is easy to keep believers from discovering and receiving it from the Lord. It is easy for the enemy to keep us focused instead on "Heroes of the Faith," living vicariously through them. We do have our moments, true, where we swoon and begin replicating the behaviors of "spiritual giants," because if it worked for them, maybe it will work for us. The reality is that it rarely, if

---

[19] 1 Peter 1:10-12

[20] Joshua 5:13-15

[21] Exodus 15:3, 6-7

ever, does, and we end up abandoning the pursuit with arrows in our backs. The arrows are the lies of the enemy, and they often sound like, "There must be something wrong with me," "God must not be able to use me," or "I just need to be more dutiful."

These lies have a consistent effect; it is the "noise" that keeps us from hearing the voice of our Father in heaven.

Our Father, the Original

It is no great secret that our concept of God is shaped by our instruction and experience. I was brought up in a home where God was presented primarily as holy and as a provider. He was presented as Jehovah-Tsidkenu (The LORD is righteousness) and Jehovah-Jireh (The LORD is our provider). Not only was He portrayed this way, but our family's approach toward Him reflected this perspective. Our prayers appealed to His provision and sustenance. We expected that God would provide, and life was full of opportunity for Him to do so. There were many occasions when we were in need and groceries would appear on our front porch, or money would come anonymously in the mail. Our perception of God was as a faithful provider, and our lifestyle backed it up. What was the result of all this? As an adult and leading my own household now, trusting God is not a foreign concept. There is no inner turmoil within me as to whether or not He will provide. That doesn't mean that I am whimsical and carefree during times of need-I am still affected by the logistics of it. But, He always provides.

Having said this, all of the provision that I experienced in God did not translate into experience of other attributes of His. I did not really understand or appreciate His grace, mercy, comfort, affection, power, authority, love, peace, etc. When I would read scriptures about those other attributes, it was always with an academic acknowledgment. In other words, I knew God loved me because I read it in the Bible, but not because I had experienced it with Him. The song of my heart may as well have been, "Jesus loves me, this I know, *for the Bible tells me so*..." Everything changed when I experienced His love firsthand.

One of the metaphors that God has long used in my learning of Him is that of a diamond. Diamonds, in all their beauty and purity, are by design multifaceted. They can only be what they are because of the abundance of their individual facets. As such, all of the individual facets function in unison to refract light, to dazzle in brilliance. One might say that a diamond models, in a diminished way, the nature of God. God is multifaceted. Just when we think we understand one facet of His divine nature, we see another one for the first time. Just when we start to pigeonhole the Almighty, we see a facet on the opposite end of the spectrum that completely baffles us and seems to be in contrast to what we had pegged Him as. We tend to "miss out" on the richness of His nature when we fail to experience all the facets He wants to reveal to us.

As we continue to mature, we start to discover, bit-by-bit, varied and increasingly complex facets of His divine nature. A big part of this is His role as our Daddy. The Aramaic word, "Abba," is used in the New Testament to describe how we ought to pray; it is the conversational word that was used to address a father. Jesus uses this word to speak to His Heavenly Father in Mark 14:36, and we are exhorted to do the same in Galatians 4:6, and again in Romans 8:15, which states, "For you have not received a spirit of slavery leading to fear again, but you have received a spirit of adoption as sons by which we cry out, 'Abba! Father!'"

When we come to know the Father as "children," we begin to bond with Him as our Daddy. It is the way any Aramaic youth would have used the word; "Abba; Daddy." As we mature spiritually into "young men (and women)" in the words of 1 John 2:13, our relationship with the Father matures more into a posture of "Abba, Dad!" Regardless of our level of maturity in the faith, knowing Him as "Abba" denotes everything that Dad/Father does in English. "Abba" was used by young Aramaic speaking children addressing their parent, as well as in solemn moments speaking *about* one's parent; it was a comprehensive term.[22]

So, let's bring it home to you and me. Ephesians 1:3-14 tells us that not only did the Heavenly Father choose us before the earth was formed, but He designed an amazing destiny for us, and He adopted us as His chosen sons (and daughters) through Jesus Christ, according to the kind intention of His will, and He has lavished upon us His grace and His inheritance. Lavished! Kind intention! These words do not portray a stingy or reluctant Father.

What a beautiful description of His affection toward us! We must yield ourselves to Him, and in spite of our barriers and our fears, it is easy, because His perfect love casts out fear. Love, not fear, begins to define the nature of our communion with our Heavenly Father.

I believe that before we can grow into our pre-ordained destiny, we must first come to know the great Adonai, the Jehovah of the Old Covenant, as our tender, compassionate Daddy. You see, we cannot very well understand our position as adopted children if we cannot come to Him as

---

[22] "Jesus in his Jewish Context," by Geza Vermes

our Daddy. If we cannot come to Him, we cannot yield ourselves completely to Him. Now, for all of us stuck in a fear-based understanding of Jehovah, yielding takes on a different meaning: surrender. We hear this word used a lot, and I think it is telling of how we see God. We surrender to a fearsome Jehovah, but we yield to our Daddy. Surrender is the language of conflict, while yielding is the language of understanding. Does this mean that surrender is a flawed concept? Absolutely not! It is, rather, indicative of our perspective of God. Surrender is necessary, but it demonstrates our understanding of *one* facet of God's characteristics. This is necessary, for this is how we understand the Gospel and our need for salvation. We must yield ourselves to Him, and in spite of our barriers and our fears, it is easy, because His perfect love casts out fear. Love, not fear, begins to define the nature of our communion with our Heavenly Father.

If the concept of the Father as "Daddy" is awkward, I can only surmise that it is because it is foreign to us. It is certainly Biblical, but why does it sound strange, especially for those of us who approach Him as our "Heavenly Father?" It is likely because we have bypassed this developmental stage of our faith. "Is that even possible?" you may ask. Sure it is! If we can, due to environmental factors, miss out on significant developmental stages in our adolescence, we can certainly miss out on similar stages in the spiritual sense. Can we function without experiencing such a stage? Absolutely. Will we know what we are missing? Probably not. However, the need for us to experience one of these formative stages generally rears its ugly head later in life, as we ultimately discover that we are missing a necessary component to functioning as a "whole" person. I believe the same is true in our faith.

CHAPTER 4

THE SOURCE OF AUTHORITY

"As I learned it was safe to yield myself to my Father, He responded by awakening my authority against the enemy and against the status quo."

"Submit therefore to God. Resist the devil and he will flee from you." James 4:7

"Humble yourselves in the presence of the Lord, and He will exalt you." James 4:10

The memorable characters of the Bible exhibited great authority. Authority is not based on a person being "dominant" or the "alpha-wolf." It is not based on natural talent. Authority is based on a few essential factors that God wants to develop in each one of our lives.

Understanding our position in the Lord

I do not simply mean knowing the classic "positional truths" of the Scriptures: I am accepted, I am loved, I am forgiven, etc. These truths get us part of the way, but they still have some distance to them. These truths tell us about our position, but they do not tell us the actual name. They do not tell us who we are. This is where many, many Christians live their lives, stuck between knowing about their position and knowing the Father's view of them. The book of Ephesians describes a Father who has specifically created us and put His mark on us, setting us apart for His timing and purpose. He has adopted us and lavished on us the things that we desperately need. He has also given us an inheritance, and as proof, He has given us a living promise ring, the Holy Spirit. You and I were sealed with the Holy Spirit of promise, who was given to us as a pledge of our inheritance![23]

It describes His intention as kind toward us. How many of us truly believe this? If we did, why would we be so fearful to encounter our Heavenly Father? We are afraid to learn His plan for our life, to find our calling, because we are certain that it will be unkind. It will be tortuous, inflicting on us a dominion and coercion to a sovereign, powerful plan that we must endure. What we fail to realize is that our Celestial Father, our Creator, has crafted us specially for the unique task He has reserved for us. We don't really believe this, do we? We believe that our relationship

---

[23] Ephesians 1:3-14

to God's will is that we are a square peg that He will certainly pound, over and over, until it fits the hole. Ladies and Gentlemen, He may need to chasten us when we go astray, but let us be crystal clear. "Calling" is the place where our puzzle piece fits into the big picture. It is where, with the perfect aim of a master sniper, we strike the bull's-eye of destiny. Calling is fulfillment, not because of how we measure success, but because we are operating in a place where our spiritual gifts, passions, experience, and strengths all align with where God is at work in the Church and the world. I know lots of people in ministry. The ones that are truly fulfilled are the ones that know beyond a shadow of doubt that they are filling the role that they, and only they, could possibly fill, because God Himself has made them for the role and the role for them. Positive results, while wonderful, are not the measure of the success of this role, but rather, the continued alignment with the will of the Father. How do we stay in tune with this? Every step of the way must be taken in tandem with the Holy Spirit, listening for His promptings and remaining ready to respond. After all, He is the one to enable us, isn't He? If we believe this, then we must stay with Him, stride by stride. This is true obedience for the mature believer: hearing the voice of God, and taking action on it.

We Believers tend to reverse the meaning of the Scripture, "To obey is better than sacrifice…" We interpret this as meaning that we should be dutiful and obedient to the rules, because that means more to God than the things we could "give up" for Him. Let's look at the full scripture in context now. "Samuel said, 'Has the LORD as much delight in burnt offerings and sacrifices as in obeying the voice of the LORD? Behold, to obey is better than sacrifice, and to heed than the fat of rams.'" 1 Samuel 15:22 This verse actually means almost the complete opposite of how we typically use it!

According to the prophet Samuel, obeying God's voice pleases Him more than our duty. Now Desiree and I come from a very cessationist Christian background, and our experience certainly fits this model. How many years did we spend finding our worth in duty and responsibility? Our aspiration was to be shining examples of Godliness to the world. We thought we were pleasing God by being so obedient, but obedient to what? We were obedient to the law, to the system, and to expectations. Is that wrong? Of course not, but it is only a building block in the infrastructure of faith. The problem comes in time as we eventually define spirituality through the concrete hallway of duty and responsibility, not yet understanding what it means to "walk in the Spirit." Isn't this what the Pharisees did?

As spiritual children, babes in Christ, we begin with childlike obedience to the simple truth of the law. After all, we will not know our need for grace unless the law points us to Jesus Christ. However, as we mature, we grow to recognize the prompting of the Holy Spirit and the voice of the Father. Our obedience switches gears during this transition, like a train switching tracks. We now must grow in responding to His invitations. What kind of invitations? "Brandon, wake up. Come away with me!" "Desiree, go to the coffee shop and wait. There is someone there for you to talk to." Obedience looks different in these moments. It is an invitation to join God where He is at work. Sure, we can brush it off, but oh, the disappointment and wondering I experience in the loss of having rejected an invitation. Authority comes from knowing you are in the Father's will, moment by moment.

Knowing who our Father created us to be

Socrates said, "Without self-knowledge, there can be no other knowledge worth having." With very few exceptions, I believe this statement to be true. It is said that inside each one of us there is a God shaped vacuum. The actual quote that this is paraphrased from is the following: "What else does this craving, and this helplessness, proclaim but that there was once in man a true happiness, of which all that now remains is the empty print and trace? This he tries in vain to fill with everything around him, seeking in things that are not there the help he cannot find in those that are, though none can help, since this infinite abyss can be filled only with an infinite and immutable object; in other words by God himself."[24]

This "vacuum" is a great hole in our heart that only God can fill. Many Western Christians, if not most, believe this hole is filled when we come to salvation. We think that once the vacuum is "filled" through salvation, we the longing is fulfilled. However, salvation is just the beginning of the story. I know many, many Christians that struggle with feeling unfulfilled and feeling guilty about it. They believe that since they have the Comforter in their heart, they shouldn't feel bad. "What is wrong with me?" In most cases I find that this despair is tied to a lack of understanding of their identity in the Lord. They don't know who they are or why they were created. How can a person experience the authority of the Lord in this state?

Emptying ourselves of our own agenda

There is no greater model of this than our Savior Himself, Jesus, the Christ. He emptied Himself, taking on the form of a servant, and was

---

[24] "Pensees," by Blaise Pascal, A. J. Krailsheimer

made in the image of a man.[25] He asserted, "I proceeded forth and have come from God, for I have not even come on My own initiative, but He sent Me."[26] Even when He was young, He had a clear sense of his need to live deliberately. Remember when He was "lost" in Jerusalem for a few days and His parents finally found Him, teaching and listening in the temple? They scolded Him for making them worry, and His response was a poignant reminder to them of what they may have forgotten, "Why did you seek Me? Did you not know that I must be about My Father's business?"[27]

It is perplexing to consider that Jesus was not here for His own agenda, but the Father's. It is strange to consider that the divine Jesus listened to and obeyed the Father. We often think of Jesus simply as God in the flesh, walking around doing miracles and *not* zapping people because He was "restraining" His power. Maybe that is why we are so confused over what it means to be "Christ-like."

Jesus' words seem to indicate a different relationship with His Father in heaven. Jesus emptied Himself of His divine attributes to become a human. He came here as a man on a mission. And from what He said, it would appear that He was only given knowledge from His Father on an "as-needed" basis. "But of that day and hour no one knows, not even the angels of heaven, nor the Son, but the Father alone."[28] It would also appear that He was only given power and authority as the Father saw fit. "You know of Jesus of Nazareth, how God anointed Him with the Holy Spirit and with power, and how He went about doing good and healing all who were oppressed by the devil, for God was with Him."[29]

Finally, it would appear that Jesus could not initiate and operate outside of what the Father directly showed Him to do. "Truly, truly, I say to you, the Son can do nothing of Himself, unless it is something He sees the Father doing; for whatever the Father does, these things the Son also does in like manner." For the Father loves the Son, and shows Him all things that He Himself is doing; and the Father will show Him greater works than these, so that you will marvel. "For just as the Father raises

---

[25] Philippians 2:7

[26] John 8:42

[27] Luke 2:48,49

[28] Matthew 24:36

[29] Acts 10:38

the dead and gives them life, even so the Son also gives life to whom He wishes. John 5:19-21

Do you hear the tender message in this last reference? "The Son," Jesus, "can do nothing of Himself, unless it is something He sees the Father doing." Does this sound a bit like mentoring? "For the Father loves the Son, and shows Him all things that He Himself is doing." The Father *loves* His Son, and as His Son, He receives authority from His Father. According to the passage we read earlier in this chapter, our Father loves us also, His adopted sons, and has authority ready to pour into us as well. What does the implementation look like? Jesus saw it modeled in the Father, activated by the Holy Spirit; even so, we must receive our identity, purpose, and authority from the Father, activated and empowered by the Holy Spirit.

The Source of Jesus's authority

According to Jesus Himself, He did not come with His own agenda. He operated out of His Father's directives. As He received instruction, He discerned, He took action. Jesus didn't need to know all the specifics. The Father would direct Him when the time was ready. This is such a pure picture of divine authority. Jesus knew exactly who He was, and He knew exactly why He was here. The rest of the story He appears to have lived out, moment by moment, in communion with the Father, listening for and responding to the voice of the Father. This is what it means to "walk in the Spirit."

Jesus was rock solid in his understanding of His authority. Jesus operated consistently out of direction from the Father and infilling by the Holy Spirit to perform the work He came to do. Nothing deterred Jesus from this state of mind. "Well sure," you say. "He was God! Of course He couldn't be shaken." Remember, however, that Jesus was flesh and blood. Do you really think Jesus never got hurt physically? Do you really think that Jesus wasn't the object of ridicule? Remember, the Bible says that Jesus was tempted in all the ways we are. "For we do not have a high priest who cannot sympathize with our weaknesses, but One who has been tempted *in all things* as we are, yet without sin."[30] This means that Jesus was tempted to respond inappropriately when threatened. He was tempted to doubt when provisions were questionable. He even questioned whether His death on the cross was the only option. "And He went a little beyond them, and fell on His face and prayed, saying, 'My Father, if it is possible, let this cup pass from Me; yet not as I will, but as

---

[30] Hebrews 4:15

You will."'[31] Yet, in all this, He did not sin. He remained in alignment with the will of the Father. "...He humbled Himself by becoming obedient to the point of death, even death on a cross." Philippians 2:8

If we look closely at the story of Legion, you will see Jesus in action in a very unique situation. A man is possessed with many demons. Some believe as many as two thousand. He is uncontrollable. He can break locks and tear chains apart. He runs out to meet Jesus:

"They came to the other side of the sea, into the country of the Gerasenes. When He got out of the boat, immediately a man from the tombs with an unclean spirit met Him, and he had his dwelling among the tombs. And no one was able to bind him anymore, even with a chain; because he had often been bound with shackles and chains, and the chains had been torn apart by him and the shackles broken in pieces, and no one was strong enough to subdue him. Constantly, night and day, he was screaming among the tombs and in the mountains, and gashing himself with stones. Seeing Jesus from a distance, he ran up and bowed down before Him; and shouting with a loud voice, he said, "What business do we have with each other, Jesus, Son of the Most High God? I implore You by God, do not torment me!" For He had been saying to him, "Come out of the man, you unclean spirit!" And He was asking him, "What is your name?" And he said to Him, "My name is Legion; for we are many." And he began to implore Him earnestly not to send them out of the country. Now there was a large herd of swine feeding nearby on the mountain. The demons implored Him, saying, "Send us into the swine so that we may enter them." Jesus gave them permission. And coming out, the unclean spirits entered the swine; and the herd rushed down the steep bank into the sea, about two thousand of them; and they were drowned in the sea." Mark 5:1-13

The detail that you must recognize here is that Jesus does not just issue a single command and have the instant obedience of the demons. Jesus had been commanding the demons to come out. How many times did He command them? We don't know. But, Jesus has the final say, as always, when He gives them permission to leave the man and enter the two thousand pigs. What would you have done if your command, in the name and authority of Jesus Christ, did not control the enemy the way you expected? Would you be rattled? Would you be shaken? Jesus stood His ground, knowing the authority He had from the Father, and the demons had to obey.

---

[31] Matthew 26:39

As Jesus approached from a distance, the man ran out to meet Him, recognizing immediately who He was. No, he did not recognize Jesus' physical appearance; he recognized the authority that Jesus carried. The demons recognized His authority. They pleaded with Him to not torment them. Again you say, "That is Jesus! Of course demons recognize His authority."

Alright, let's look at another example. God was performing extraordinary miracles by the hands of Paul, so that handkerchiefs or aprons were even carried from his body to the sick, and the diseases left them and the evil spirits went out. But also some of the Jewish exorcists, who went from place to place, attempted to name over those who had the evil spirits the name of the Lord Jesus, saying, "I adjure you by Jesus whom Paul preaches." Seven sons of one Sceva, a Jewish chief priest, were doing this. Acts 19:11-14

These men, Jewish exorcists, were operating without authority from God. They were trying to use a formula that they saw work in the ministry of the apostles. They tried to use a sort of "third-party" authority, casting out demons in the name of the Jesus that Paul spoke of. The outcome was disastrous.

"And the evil spirit answered and said to them, 'I recognize Jesus, and I know about Paul, but who are you?' And the man, in whom was the evil spirit, leaped on them and subdued all of them and overpowered them, so that they fled out of that house naked and wounded." Acts 19:15, 16

Do demons know who you are?

Authority with Humility

As you get to know your Father, you get to know His heart. You come to understand His business, as well as your role in it. And inevitably, as you begin to understand how He designed you for that role, you begin to recognize the authority He has given you. You embrace it and begin to walk boldly as a light in the midst of darkness, listening for His prompting and taking action on it, and you see Him do incredible things as you obey. When we live this way, we are bound to bump up against an unexpected element; how is a person to remain humble as they move in such authority? How do you wield "command presence" and submission at the same time?

As a mentor of ours, Susan Jerome, says, authority and meekness are nearly synonymous. Both words require an emptying of self before God. Both denote submission to His will. Both attitudes operate in tandem;

there is no God-given authority outside of submission to His will and alignment with His workings.

As we grow in maturity, a truth that becomes unavoidable is the fact that, "Post-Fall," we are dead spiritually, and as a result, we no longer "know" through our spirit. So, due to the fall of mankind in the Garden of Eden, we are relegated to knowing "chiefly in the mind." Our intellect has become the filter for our existence. What is the problem with this? Well, if we are to truly know the Father, we must know Him in spirit. After all, He is not intellect, He is spirit. He very clearly *has* intellect, but He *is* spirit.[32]

If we are called to worship in spirit, pray in spirit, and walk in the spirit, how can we do so if we do not first learn to distinguish our newly quickened spirits?

Before salvation, we are dead in spirit, but alive in our intellect. In salvation, we are made alive spiritually,[33] yet it is very difficult to break out of our own rationale and mode of thought. Are we to abandon our intellect? By no means, my friends. It is through our intellect that we build the foundation of scriptural knowledge, and this is vital, because our intellect is our "Post-Fall" default way of "knowing." What we must learn to do is to give our spirit a voice. It is important to note that our spirit, made alive by the saving work of the Holy Spirit, is aligned with and in tune with the Holy Spirit, which means that it is at odds with our flesh. Our spirit, now alive in Christ, will always side with the will of the Father, and rejoices in this constant communion. When we learn to distinguish between our flesh and our spirit, when we learn to discern and "test the spirits"(including our own), we begin to give our spirit a voice, just as King David, a man after God's heart, actively did throughout Scripture.

"I call to remembrance my song in the night; I meditate within my heart, and my spirit makes diligent search."[34]

When he speaks of his heart or his spirit, the author is not speaking about his emotions. Notice that in Psalm 103:4, his spirit *experiences* emotion, as does his heart. He is not simply talking about the way his flesh feels, or the way his senses have reacted to something. He is giving his spirit a platform to be heard.

---

[32] John 4:23,24

[33] 1 Peter 3:18

[34] Psalm 77:6 New King James Version

Why does this matter? It matters because to yield our agendas and perspectives to the Father means to allow our spirit's agreement and alignment with the Father to become more powerful than our limited intellect. Our spirit has no problem trusting the Father. Our intellect does. Our spirit rejoices at the promptings and invitations of the Holy Spirit. Our intellect doubts and questions.

Encouragement

So, what happens when you begin to live with a sense of authority, yielding continually to the Father, agreeing in your spirit with His Spirit? While you, no doubt, will be transformed and invigorated by this new aspect of life, people that have known you for a long time may be skeptical. "We know the old John. He's off on some kick now…" Family may find it hard to embrace the change. The "you" that they raised, developed, nurtured and trained has become a "you" that they do not recognize. Be encouraged, because Jesus experienced the same thing. In Luke 4:14-32, Jesus emerges into His ministry and makes His mission known in the synagogue by reading from the scroll of Isaiah and announcing, "Today this Scripture has been fulfilled in your hearing." Wow! What authority! Yet He reminds us that no prophet is welcome in his hometown, and the people in the synagogue that day were no exception.

How did Jesus respond to the hostility? He removed Himself from people that wouldn't receive Him and continued on in authority. He gave His disciples the same instruction. "Any place that does not receive you or listen to you, as you go out from there, shake the dust off the soles of your feet for a testimony against them." They went out and preached that men should repent. And they were casting out many demons and were anointing with oil many sick people and healing them." Mark 6:11-13

Jesus was all about the mission. Everything He did pointed toward that end. In this focus His authority and empowerment was applied. It is no coincidence that Paul says, "I do all things for the sake of the gospel, so that I may become a fellow partaker of it." Paul was all about the mission also. He did everything for the sake of the gospel. Isn't that what we have been commissioned to? We are also to be singular in focus-the spread of the gospel. This is in alignment with the heart of God. This is why He empowers and grants authority.

Jesus laid out the challenge to you and to me when He said, "Not everyone who says to Me, 'Lord, Lord,' shall enter the kingdom of heaven, but he who does the will of My Father in heaven." Matthew 7:21

Do you walk in authority?

"...These things speak and exhort and reprove with all authority. Let no one disregard you." Titus 2:15

Chapter 5

Joining the Holy Spirit

"I was afraid of the unknown. I was afraid of 'getting it wrong.' And, I was pretty sure that I had seen the Holy Spirit misrepresented more often than not."

It is difficult to imagine walking in authority when we are full of fear. Human beings have always been afraid of the unknown, and Christians are no exception to the rule. For many of us, this applies most to our interaction with God. Many of my own fears about "experiencing" the Holy Spirit were based on stories I had heard from other people, as well as observations I had made in different churches over the years.

In this chapter, we want to talk about what it looks like to *join* the Holy Spirit-not necessarily what it looks like to *experience* Him. Let me explain the difference. When people talk about experiencing the Holy Spirit, what is often conveyed is that He Himself is an experience. He is portrayed as a product, something we can acquire and accumulate. Any pursuit of Him ends up becoming a pursuit of the symptoms of His activity, and this completely misses the point of His work. And, if we miss the point, it means that we are not in agreement and alignment with Him, which unfortunately means that we will miss out on joining Him where He is at work. Joining the Holy Spirit is a different thing altogether. If a desire to experience the Holy Spirit is born out of our own agenda, then we could say that joining him is all about His agenda. On a very basic level, we begin to join the Holy Spirit when we listen to God's voice in our hearts; we will talk more about hearing Him in this chapter. As we grow deeper in our hearing, however, joining evolves into God's invitation for us to yield of ourselves-emptying our own agendas so we can embrace His. Joining is essentially our yielding to the Holy Spirit.

Our story, however, is not one-sided. We know that we are invited to get close to God, but we also are told that He gets close with us.[35] In other words, He also joins us! The Holy Spirit makes His home with our spirit, at our core, in the hidden places where we are our truest, but where we are also most vulnerable and shut away from interaction with ourselves, with others, and with God. It is at this core within us that He tends to our wounds, gradually increasing our awareness of them and of their need for healing. The Holy Spirit joins me where I am at, and He tenderly works within me, like a master archaeologist, carefully dusting away the

---

[35] James 4:8

layers that time has deposited over my heart, all so He can restore it to the brilliance He designed in it in the first place.

To join with the Holy Spirit is both an internal and external phenomenon. As He joins us where we are at, He restores and renews our feeble hearts into relationship with our Father. And, as we join Him, we follow Him where He directs, and we take action when He indicates. This is how we live out our role in the kingdom of heaven. In both cases, the joining is all about knowing the Father more intimately: knowing His thoughts toward us, knowing His heart toward the world, and knowing Him so well that, like Moses, our faces and hearts reflect the glow of His glory. The more we know Him, the more we know faith, understanding, wisdom, worship, and adoration.

The agenda of the Holy Spirit

We must remember that the emphasis of the Spirit of God is two-fold: pointing the lost to Jesus Christ, and uniting believers to the Father. He is not in the business of drawing attention unto Himself, so any ministry that makes it a goal to *experience* the Holy Spirit specifically has already got an agenda that is contrary to the Spirit's.

The Holy Spirit invites us into the Father's desire. This is where we get to know our Father. This is where we get to know His thoughts toward us. This is where His tenderness toward us endears us to Him, and inspires us to call Him "Daddy," or "Papa," our modern way of saying "Abba." This is where we get to know who He says we are. This is where we get to know what He designed and impassioned us to do for the rest of our existence. It is with our Papa that we finally understand the meaning for our existence. This all occurs as we hear our Father speak through the conduit of the Holy Spirit.

What is it like to hear from God? Our experience is that there are two elements to hearing from God. One element is *how* He speaks to each one of us, and the second element is *what* He speaks. As we grow into maturity, we will experience both the *how* and the *what* in much deeper, more thorough ways. Let's take a look at these two equally important elements of hearing from God.

How God speaks to us through the Holy Spirit

Some Christians have a hard time with the notion of hearing from God. Part of the misconception is that hearing must involve our ears, because people assume that we are talking about an audible voice from heaven. And, while certain characters throughout the Scriptures did hear God this way, they appear to be in the minority. Most of the time, God speaks to His children internally. What does this mean?

God speaks to us through His Holy Spirit within us. His Spirit communes with our spirit, and through this connection, our channel to the Father's voice is opened. Learning to recognize His voice is a lot like tuning in to a faint radio station. It is hard to hear sometimes. It is hard to understand sometimes. The signal seems to disappear completely at other times. And sometimes, it is bright and clear.

Sometimes, the Holy Spirit gives us a sense. It may be an understanding of the Lord's presence with us in a difficult circumstance. The Holy Spirit may give us a word. It is commonly a specific message for a specific situation. Frequently, the Holy Spirit will give us a metaphor. It can be a picture in our mind, a song, a daydream, or any other mode of communicating something to us that He wants us to understand. Often, the Holy Spirit gives us a prompting. It may be one of those moments where you are feeling a strong sense that He wants you to go out of your way to a different grocery store than you normally go to in order to minister to someone there. Commonly, the Holy Spirit gives us an invitation. Perhaps it is an understanding that He is inviting us to fast. Finally, the Holy Spirit gives us imperatives. An imperative can feel like an urgent need to take action.

The reality is that God speaks to us all the time, but we don't recognize it as Him. We often take credit for inspiration that comes from Him. We claim His ideas as our own. I believe that not only do we need to acknowledge that He speaks, but we need to learn to give Him the credit far more often than we do. When we don't acknowledge and credit Him accordingly, we keep Him at arms length.

Acknowledging Him, however, is not where we stop. Hearing also requires understanding. Part of getting to know Him is getting His confirmation from Scripture. We get acquainted with Him more and more as we gain understanding of His communication. Conversational dialogue with our Father, while still profound, tends to be simple and clear. I am talking about those moments throughout the day where I just tell Him what I'm thinking, feeling, needing, appreciating, pondering, etc, and He responds with His perspectives. But, there are also the moments where He communicates something that I don't fully understand at the moment. Sometimes months pass before I truly understand what He is wanting me to understand. Oftentimes, He uses other Christians, Sunday sermons, and other reinforcement, to continually build and strengthen the point He is wanting to make.

Even among Christians that don't believe that God speaks directly to His children anymore, most would agree that they have been "prompted" by God to share a scripture or a specific word of encouragement with a friend. These are valid examples of how God sometimes speaks to us. The fact that the person responded to God's prompting and shared a scripture or a word with someone is another way that God speaks; He often speaks to us through other believers. This occurs even in the most conservative of churches, yet we fail to recognize these moments as God speaking to us.

I ran into a friend from a different church recently. After briefly catching up, she shared with me that she had been praying for God to heal her mind, and asked if I would remember her in prayer as well. I felt like God wanted me to pray for her right then and there, and she accepted the offer. As I prayed, I sensed that God wanted me to pray for her to receive some specific things: clarity, focus, and finally, resolve. Resolve? I hesitated before even praying the word aloud. Resolve didn't fit the evidence of a healthy mind. I actually ended up listing the word "resolve" a bit quieter, thinking that perhaps we would just gloss over it and move on. Ironically, as soon as I prayed for her to receive it, she chuckled! She shared with me that she had recently been talking to the Lord about her desire to be more resolved, and that this word had been a theme in her life all week.

Now, it would be easy to simply attribute the use of that word to coincidence. But, the reality is that God spoke to me as I was praying. He told me what to ask for. He gave me the words "clarity, focus, and resolve." I was able to celebrate God's goodness with this friend *because* we gave Him the credit for it.

Now, I must admit that this kind of interaction with the Lord and another person is relatively new to me. I've only been living this way for about ten years. Prior to that, I wouldn't have imagined that this was possible. In fact, I distinctly remember being told from the pulpit, "If anyone ever says to you that they have a word from the Lord for you, don't believe them. It is from the devil." Tragically, this message shaped my formative years as a Christian and I missed out on many years of communion with the Father and with the Body as a result.

What God says to us through the Holy Spirit

We've talked about the how, and now for the what. What is God's intent when He speaks to us? He speaks because He knows exactly what we need at our core, and He wants to minister to us in our deepest need. That is where the Holy Spirit is centered within us, and that is the place where He intercedes on our behalf to our Father. The Father agrees with the Spirit's requests, because They are One. What the Spirit prays for, the Father grants. Much of what follows has to do with *our* level of agreement with Them.

God's messages to us are based on two things: what He knows we need, and how He invites us to join Him. Sometimes we need comfort, sometimes correction, sometimes rest, shaping, or understanding. He can accomplish this through an epiphany, or even through a song. But, the most poignant ministry of the Holy Spirit happens when we are quiet and still with Him.

I had been going through an extremely difficult time with my business. It had been three months of crisis, and despite my repeated pleadings, God did not rescue me. I was at my wits end. The anxiety had given way to exhaustion, and the exhaustion had given way to numbness. I needed divine intervention.

That is when God woke me up during the night. It was 4 AM, and I was awake. I am never awake at that time unless God is inviting me to be with Him, and this was one of those nights. It had been a while, but I recognized His invitation immediately. "Come be with Me," I could hear in my mind. I went downstairs, grabbed my Bible and a pen and paper, and as I normally do in those moments, I said, "Hi Papa, I'm here. What do you want to talk about?"

Over the next hour, He showed me why He wasn't rescuing me. He gave me Scripture to explain to me that the purpose of this trial was to be a defining moment toward my destiny. He then brought back a memory from six months prior when a brother at church had given me a word of encouragement about this (yet unforeseen) coming trial. I had forgotten all about it! He then brought to my mind several "small" ways that He had provided for me, answered my prayer for wisdom, and protected me. Finally, He showed me metaphorical pictures in my mind of promises He was giving me. What kinds of messages did I receive from my Father that night? I received encouragement, promise, purpose, clarity, and perhaps most of all, a reminder that He is deeply invested in my development.

I think God likes to speak to us in the night, just like He did with the young Samuel, because our faculties are restricted. I believe that He likes to train us to hear His voice during the night hours, when there are no distractions, and when our minds are so groggy that they are "out of the way," so to speak.

Hearing is not the ultimate goal

We've talked about the *how* and the *what* of God's voice, but we really need to understand a significant truth: Hearing the voice of God is not a mark of your spirituality! So many Christians take the perspective that a person claiming to hear from God is either: crazy, immature, lying, or, if they believe the person, that person must be a "spiritual giant." The reality is that God does not speak to certain "elite" of His children, and the Scriptures are quite clear on this matter.

Among the people in the Bible who could be called part of "God's people," Cain, Jonah, Balaam, and Judas are each men who were rebellious toward God, yet He still spoke with them, and throughout their acts of sin at that! And, if that isn't enough testimony for you, consider Nebuchadnezzar, Cyrus, Abimelech, Hagar, and Cornelius-*none* of whom were of "God's people," yet God specifically spoke with them and interacted with them for His purposes. How much more so for you and me, who have the Holy Spirit residing within us as a guarantee that we are His children!

I recently spent some time with two friends from Church. One friend, "Jimmy," had been stuck for a long time. He had spent years-decades really, being controlled by guilt and shame. Jimmy would say that he doesn't hear from God as often as our other friend, "Peter." Peter often speaks of the small ways that God speaks into his day, inspiring and encouraging him.

In the past year, Jimmy had pursued prayer counseling in order move past the barriers in his relationship with God. And, the day we met, Jimmy recounted to us several profound experiences with God that radically transformed his perspectives of Him, and that brought healing to some very old wounds.

What Jimmy was assuming all along is that breadth and depth occur at the same time as we hear from God, but this is not necessarily true. The reality is that Jimmy has now experienced certain depths with the Father that Peter has not. Peter has more practice in hearing, but Jimmy has been more greatly impacted by what he has heard.

Hearing from God does not mean that you are holier than other people. It doesn't guarantee that you won't act like an idiot.[36] It doesn't mean that you won't choose sinfulness.[37] It does not ensure that you will grow spiritually.[38] It does not make you special. Hearing your Father's voice is simply a a result of the Holy Spirit residing within us.

Yet, many Christians are fearful of this notion. Why do we fear hearing from God? There are many, many reasons. Perhaps one of these reasons resonates with you: we fear that He will be displeased with us; we fear what His tone will be like; we fear that we will hear Him "wrong;" we fear what others will say; we fear that He will not answer; we fear that He will tell us to do something "crazy," like move to Africa; we fear "giving in" to an ethereal, emotionally connected way of life; we fear that it will make us behave like another denomination; and we fear that we are not spiritual enough. In great part, we fear the unknown. We fear what has not been modeled to us properly!

What it is like to experience the Holy Spirit directly

There are a few different ways that we directly experience the Holy Spirit. Hearing, as we have talked about, but we also experience the Spirit *bearing witness* within us, and finally, we can experience *the presence of the Spirit of God.*

Bearing Witness
According to 1 John 5, the Holy Spirit bears witness both in heaven and on earth. The Father and Son bear witness in heaven, and men bear witness on earth. It is only the Holy Spirit that connects the two realms. What exactly does it mean to *bear witness*, and how does the Holy Spirit do it?

Thayer defines bearing witness as "giving testimony of an actual experience, knowing something by divine revelation, not withholding testimony, and giving a good report." From this, we could say that a practical way the Holy Spirit bears witness is when He affirms within us whether an experience is from Him or not. When the Holy Spirit bears witness, we get a sense of agreement in our heart with what we are observing. When the Spirit does not bear witness, we get a sense of

---

[36] Galatians 2:11-14

[37] Hebrews 6

[38] 2 Timothy 4:10

uneasiness or anxiousness over what we are observing. Many Christians describe it as having a "creepy" feeling about what is taking place. Have you ever felt this way?

As we move forward, we will examine some of the authentic working of the Holy Spirit, and we will contrast it with the cheap knock-offs that Christians often get sucked into. This next example fits within these parameters.

I know, first hand, what it is like to be in the presence of God and to be ministered to by Him. He knows what I need, every time. Sometimes He gives me a great sense of peace. Sometimes it is an epiphany. It is whatever He decides. I was talking with a friend recently who comes from a dark background, full of self-loathing and abuse of her body. As the Lord has brought her into a place of delight and joy, and calls her out of the dark lies that once clouded her, she says that she is often struck by His kindness, His knack for using "coincidence" to His advantage, and His sense of humor. She says that often, in her tender moments with the Father, she finds herself giggling over these endearing ways that He ministers to her.

As she shared this with me, the Holy Spirit welled up a sense of agreement within me. Have I ever experienced giggling with my Father? No. But, I know how personal He is with me, and it absolutely fits what I have experienced to be true of intimate moments with Him. The Holy Spirit bore witness within me at her words. But, this is the point where the story turns.

She went on to share that other Christians were starting to ask her "how" to experience this giggling for themselves. As soon as the words were spoken, the Holy Spirit immediately stopped bearing witness within me-I felt a disagreement, an unsettled feeling in my gut. What had started as a genuine result of worship and connection with the Father was in danger of becoming a formula for other Christians to pursue an experience, rather than the Father Himself. I had to say something, and praise be to God, He illuminated the hazard before it materialized.

Experiencing the presence of the Holy Spirit
Another way that we experience the Holy Spirit is when He makes His presence known to us. There is no formula to "get the feeling." If you happen to sense His presence during a time of worship and then try to duplicate it, you are pretty much guaranteed that the effort will fall flat on its face. What works one time probably won't work the next. I think that this is His way of keeping a checks-and-balances within us, because He

knows we are likely to try to duplicate an experience, and forget that our original intent was to worship the Father!

For those that are concerned about trusting our feelings and our senses, you can always ask the Lord to confirm what you are experiencing with Scripture. As you keep asking, day by day, event by event, and moment by moment, you get to know how He responds, His tone, and the things He is concerned with and passionate about.

What is it like to sense the presence of the Holy Spirit? People commonly describe the same thing: it is a feeling of electricity running through your body, like an intense tingling on your skin. It is not an annoying sensation, nor is it pleasurable. It is simply an evidence. It is an evidence of His local and His deliberate presence. There also seems to be an intentionality to this sensation. When my foot falls asleep, it develops an annoying tingling sensation as the blood flow returns to the muscles. The tingling is isolated to my foot because that is what was affected. However, when the Holy Spirit makes His presence known, the buzzing sensation tends to migrate over my body. I may feel it start on the top of my head and make its way to my core. I may feel it moving across my back and down to my hand.

What is the purpose of this? I can only speak from experience. When I receive this indication of the Spirit's presence, it validates what the Father is doing in me, speaking to me, or starting to reveal. It is always at the opportune moment-a moment where the Father knows I need reinforcement. The Spirit's touch makes the Father's comfort very real. The Spirit's touch affirms a new direction the Father seems to be leading me in. The Holy Spirit and the Father are working off of the same shared agenda, and their ministry is complimentary.

Another way the Spirit evidences Himself to us is in the ministry of healing. The Father has directed Desiree on multiple occasions to heal people. In her case, the Holy Spirit brings a warmth into her hands as she steps out in faith. The sensation of heat serves to reaffirm her faith and propel her forward in the will of the Father as she obeys Him and lays hands on a person and the Holy Spirit heals through her. Once again, the work of the Spirit fuels and facilitates the Father's agenda.

Why we join the Holy Spirit

The Father is concerned with uniting His children, after all, we are together the Bride of His Son. The genuine work of the Holy Spirit links His children together as we care for each other, speak truth to each other, and as we worship Him together through our shared experiences in service, sacrifice and suffering. When we are renovated by the work of the Comforter within us, it answers our isolation, our loneliness, and our fear, and in turn, we become consumed by the longing to help others find the same healing. We become ambassadors of reconciliation.[39]

The Father also gives us His Spirit because without Him, our knowledge and works won't generate healthy fruit. Dying trees can produce fruit even as they decline, but the fruit is inedible. 1 Corinthians 13 reminds us of the annoyance and emptiness of our "righteous" deeds when they lack the genuine love and passion that only the Holy Spirit can inspire within us. When we grow in the Spirit, we gain His perspective, His compassion, and His grace.

Many people lump the gifts of the Spirit into the category of experiencing the Holy Spirit. We must not confuse the two. Any encounter with the Holy Spirit must be recognized as an invitation or direction into the Father's presence. Gifts of the Spirit are only the symptoms of that communion. Therefore, being "Spirit-filled" is most accurately a description of being yielded to and joined with the Spirit, and of being in communion with the Father. Gifting may automatically occur as He leads, but it may not. It could be worship. It could be singing. It could be journaling. It could be any number of things that the Father asks or inspires. They all, including the gifts, are only the response to communion with Him. Far too often we see Christians try to practice the gifts with no concept of what it means to be in communion with the Father through the Holy Spirit. It is a case of putting the cart before the horse!

How to begin to join the Holy Spirit

Our experience with this question comes down to one answer: *We must ask the Father to fill us with His Spirit*. It was only after this point that I started to move into this territory. Beforehand, I really didn't have any desire to pursue God this way. I was content with theology and debating. I was content with my performance. But gradually it was replaced by a deep discontent. I thought the discontent was toward Christianity, but it wasn't. It was toward my *dead* Christianity. I desperately needed God to make Himself real in my life-I needed proof that I hadn't wasted decades believing some archaic concept of God. It was in this desperation that I cried out to God, and I kept crying out to Him to fill me with His Spirit. I didn't know what it would look like, but I was pretty sure I knew what it shouldn't look like. I felt safe, theologically speaking, to ask for "filling."

---

[39] 2 Corinthians 5:18

And sure enough, as He always does, God answers "yes" to that genuine and pure pleading, because it is aligned with His desire. It didn't happen right away. It felt like I begged and pleaded for a long, long time. God was already working, but He was also allowing me to reach the breaking point of my desperation so that when I finally did recognize the fresh activity of the Holy Spirit, I couldn't take any credit for it. There was no life left in me up until that point, and therefore, any glimmer of spirituality could only be credited to Him.

When you begin to pray in expectation of a response from your Father, I would recommend journaling your prayers and jotting down the "thoughts" that come to your mind as you pray. When you talk to your Father, what are your expectations? What are your afraid of? What are you ashamed of? Write it all down. What does Scripture have to say about those fears and perspectives? Write it down. Assume that the Holy Spirit will begin to illuminate the Scriptures to you and will speak directly to you through them. I would ask God to further confirm these concepts in your pastor's sermons and in the Christians that speak truth into your life.

These are all safe ways that we can develop and exercise our hearing. And as you grow in these practices, you will begin to notice additional ways that God confirms His truths to you. You will begin to recognize how His messages sound and what the tone of His communication is. As you begin to become familiar with His ways, it will become easier to distinguish what is from Him and what is not. It all begins with us asking in belief.

Son, how do you think God talks to His children?
"He uses our hearts instead of email."-Aidan

CHAPTER 6

ESSENTIAL ROLES OF THE HOLY SPIRIT

"I began to realize how much I feared and misunderstood the Holy Spirit, and that my disbelief had restricted His activity in my heart."

The Holy Spirit is not a cloud of fairy dust. He is the active representation of God, the conduit for His communication, and the fuel for His fire. While He has been called by many names throughout the Scriptures, the Holy Spirit is creative, powerful, and the most interactive part of the Trinity, from a human perspective.

The Spirit has a "personality" of sorts, in as much as He can be offended and can experience emotion, like jealousy. The Spirit of God is self-aware, and as such, has person-hood. The Holy Spirit occupies many roles and in many ways.

In this chapter we will look at the primary roles of the Holy Spirit in the world, in the Kingdom of God, in the Church, and finally, in the Christian. The intent of this chapter is to demonstrate all the different roles, behaviors and activities the Bible shows the Holy Spirit engaging in. We believe it is important to explore this thoroughly, as we too often limit the Holy Spirit to the picture we have of Him in our minds. Some of us don't believe He does what the Scriptures describe Him doing, while others attribute far more activity to Him than the Bible depicts. The Holy Spirit does more than just convict us of sin, and He certainly does more than indwell us at the point of salvation. If you, the reader, do not believe in the activity of the Holy Spirit in a certain capacity, our hope is that you will be encouraged and blessed by discovering all the other comprehensive ways the Holy Spirit operates in the world today. In other words, we want to remind ourselves of how robust He truly is. Please bear this in mind as you proceed.

The Holy Spirit as the Spirit of God

"Therefore I make known to you that no one speaking by the Spirit of God says, 'Jesus is accursed;' and no one can say, 'Jesus is Lord,' except by the Holy Spirit." 1 Corinthians 12:3

The Spirit of God is the first Biblical reference that is made to the Holy Spirit. The opening verse of the Hebrew Scriptures names God as Elohim, a name that denotes plurality. We recall in Genesis 1:26 that God states, "Let Us make man in Our image." Critics state that mankind, who at this time was either monotheistic or polytheistic, was too primitive to create such a complex notion of God, a supposed blend of mono and polytheism into one God that fit both descriptions. Christians, on the other hand, believe in the active roles that the Godhead played during the creation of the world and subsequent events throughout the Scriptures. Here are a few roles the Spirit of God played throughout the pages of history.

Creating
"Then God said, 'Let Us make man in Our image, according to Our likeness; and let them rule over the fish of the sea and over the birds of the sky and over the cattle and over all the earth, and over every creeping thing that creeps on the earth.'" Genesis 1:26

"The Spirit of God has made me, And the breath of the Almighty gives me life." Job 33:4

Patrolling
"The earth was formless and void, and darkness was over the surface of the deep, and the Spirit of God was moving over the surface of the waters." Genesis 1:2

As an interesting side note, the original Hebrew uses the word "vibrating" over the face of the deep. In this context, some believe the Spirit to play an energizing, activating role in the creation of the world.

Anointing
"Do not cast me away from Your presence and do not take Your Holy Spirit from me." Psalms 51:11

"You know of Jesus of Nazareth, how God anointed Him with the Holy Spirit and with power, and how He went about doing good and healing all who were oppressed by the devil, for God was with Him." Acts 10:38

Intervening in the Natural Order
"Now the birth of Jesus Christ was as follows: when His mother Mary had been betrothed to Joseph, before they came together she was found to be with child by the Holy Spirit." Matthew 1:18

The Spirit of God is our introduction to the Holy Spirit in the Bible. The very first activities described of Him are the ones of action: active involvement in the creation, development and operation of the created realm.

The Holy Spirit as the Spirit of Judgment

"When the Lord has washed away the filth of the daughters of Zion and purged the bloodshed of Jerusalem from her midst, by the Spirit of judgment and the Spirit of burning..." Isaiah 4:4

The Holy Spirit has a judiciary quality to His nature. His sense of good and evil can be appealed to or offended, and employed by God to dispense justice. Here are some verses that describe the activity of the Spirit of Judgment.

Convicts
"And He, when He comes, will convict the world concerning sin and righteousness and judgment; concerning sin, because they do not believe in Me; and concerning righteousness, because I go to the Father and you no longer see Me; and concerning judgment, because the ruler of this world has been judged." John 16:8-11

"...For our gospel did not come to you in word only, but also in power and in the Holy Spirit and with full conviction; just as you know what kind of men we proved to be among you for your sake." 1 Thessalonians 1:5

The Holy Spirit as the Spirit of judgment convicts the world: calling to account, and exposing our fault. It is in this context that Paul writes these words, "Therefore the Law has become our tutor to lead us to Christ..." The Holy Spirit shows us our sin by comparing our righteousness to that of the Law, and since we cannot measure up, He ushers us to Jesus Christ who is our only way into eternal life.

The Holy Spirit as the Spirit of Burning

"When the Lord has washed away the filth of the daughters of Zion and purged the bloodshed of Jerusalem from her midst, by the Spirit of judgment and the Spirit of burning..." Isaiah 4:4

I believe that when the Bible speaks of the purifying, refining and renewing work of the Lord, that it is the Holy Spirit that facilitates this process.

Purifies
"He will sit as a smelter and purifier of silver, and He will purify the sons of Levi and refine them like gold and silver, so that they may present to the LORD offerings in righteousness." Malachi 3:3

Refines
"For You have tried us, O God; You have refined us as silver is refined." Psalms 66:10

Renews
"He saved us, not on the basis of deeds which we have done in righteousness, but according to His mercy, by the washing of regeneration and renewing by the Holy Spirit..." Titus 3:5

The Holy Spirit is actively engaged in refining us-purifying us of our impurities. What are those impurities? I believe they are our perspectives, our agendas, our self-medications-all the things that generate sin in our lives. Christians tend to view the impurities as the sins themselves, but the real evidence of refining comes when our former wounds no longer drive us repeatedly back to those sins.

The Holy Spirit as the Spirit of Jesus

"...And the Holy Spirit descended upon Him in bodily form like a dove, and a voice came out of heaven, 'You are My beloved Son, in You I am well-pleased.'" Luke 3:22

"...And after they came to Mysia, they were trying to go into Bithynia, and the Spirit of Jesus did not permit them..." Acts 16:7

"...For I know that this will turn out for my deliverance through your prayers and the provision of the Spirit of Jesus Christ, according to my earnest expectation and hope, that I will not be put to shame in anything, but that with all boldness, Christ will even now, as always, be exalted in my body, whether by life or by death." Philippians 1:19,20

When it comes to the Holy Spirit in the role of the Spirit of Jesus, we look at how the Spirit appeared and was portrayed most actively in Jesus. During His time as a man, Jesus was yielded to the Father, and the Holy Spirit enabled, empowered and ministered to Him and through Him as a result.

Can be seen
"I did not recognize Him, but He who sent me to baptize in water said to me, 'He upon whom you see the Spirit descending and remaining upon Him, this is the One who baptizes in the Holy Spirit.'" John 1:33

Can be heard *(externally)*
"When the day of Pentecost had come, they were all together in one place. And suddenly there came from heaven a noise like a violent

rushing wind, and it filled the whole house where they were sitting. And there appeared to them tongues as of fire distributing themselves, and they rested on each one of them. And they were all filled with the Holy Spirit and began to speak with other tongues, as the Spirit was giving them utterance." Acts 2:1-4

Can be heard *(internally)*
"Therefore, just as the Holy Spirit says, 'TODAY IF YOU HEAR HIS VOICE...'" Hebrews 3:7

"While they were ministering to the Lord and fasting, the Holy Spirit said, 'Set apart for Me Barnabas and Saul for the work to which I have called them.'" Acts 13:2

"And coming to us, he took Paul's belt and bound his own feet and hands, and said, 'This is what the Holy Spirit says: 'In this way the Jews at Jerusalem will bind the man who owns this belt and deliver him into the hands of the Gentiles.'" Acts 21:11

The "Spirit of Jesus" sounds like a conflicting term, doesn't it? Why would the disciples use this terminology? I believe it is simply because Jesus was the first to model to them what it looked like to be filled with the Spirit. And until Jesus began to teach them about the "Comforter" that He was going to leave with them, they probably assumed that Jesus was doing all of His works of His own power. They saw the Holy Spirit descend on Jesus when John baptized Him, and immediately afterward, Jesus began to perform miracles and to move in authority. They called the Holy Spirit the Spirit of Jesus because they were emulating their mentor.

The Holy Spirit as the Comforter

"And I will pray the Father, and he shall give you another Comforter, that he may abide with you for ever; Even the Spirit of truth; whom the world cannot receive, because it seeth him not, neither knoweth him: but ye know him; for he dwelleth with you, and shall be in you. I will not leave you comfortless: I will come to you." John 14:16-18 KJV

When Jesus said, "Peace I leave with you; My peace I give to you; not as the world gives do I give to you. Do not let your heart be troubled, nor let it be fearful," He was speaking of the work of The Comforter. The Spirit joins us, in this role, with encouraging "togetherness" that is meant to bolster, reinforce, and calm our hearts. Here are some of the ways the Spirit does this work:

Flourishes hope
"Now may the God of hope fill you with all joy and peace in believing, so that you will abound in hope by the power of the Holy Spirit." Romans 15:13

Enables fellowship
"The grace of the Lord Jesus Christ, and the love of God, and the fellowship of the Holy Spirit, be with you all." 2 Corinthians 13:14

Sustains joy
"You also became imitators of us and of the Lord, having received the word in much tribulation with the joy of the Holy Spirit..." 1 Thessalonians 1:6

Comforts
"So the church throughout all Judea and Galilee and Samaria enjoyed peace, being built up; and going on in the fear of the Lord and in the comfort of the Holy Spirit, it continued to increase." Acts 9:31

It is our knee-jerk reaction as devout, "rooted-in-knowledge" Evangelicals, to relegate this office of the Holy Spirit to those people we deem as needy or immature in the faith. After all, "Greater is He that is in you than He that is in the world," right? We tend to elevate people that "transcend" the trappings of human emotion as "mature" and therefore, "healthy." But, this is not at all what the Bible teaches. Listen to the following passage from Isaiah 61 that summarizes the mission of the Messiah:

"The Spirit of the Lord God is upon me, because the Lord has anointed me to bring good news to the afflicted; He has sent me to bind up the brokenhearted, to proclaim liberty to captives and freedom to prisoners; to proclaim the favorable year of the LORD and the day of vengeance of our God; to comfort all who mourn, to grant those who mourn in Zion, giving them a garland instead of ashes, the oil of gladness instead of mourning, the mantle of praise instead of a s spirit of fainting..."

This passage speaks repeatedly about God, the Trinity, working together to comfort, to heal, to rescue, to avenge, to revive and to bring joy to His people. His plan for salvation was not a dry, academic acknowledgement of sin and rescue from death. Rather, He intended for our emotional needs to be met in the actions of the Messiah, our great Savior, and our emotional wholeness was meant to go hand in hand with our salvation from hell.

If our Father in Heaven were to minimize our need for inner healing-the healing of our hearts, not only would it contradict Jesus' mission, but it would belittle our deepest needs. Furthermore, for the Father to leave us brokenhearted, it would prove to humanity that God is emotionally disconnected and uninvolved. After all, we are made in His image; like Father, like sons and daughters.

The reality is that God-Father, Son and Spirit, are deeply invested in our wholeness:
- They recognize our brokenness
- They care profoundly
- They do not minimize our pain or need for healing
- They work to illuminate our areas of brokenness
- They work to restore those areas of wounding

Even now, you may not have any problem accepting that this is true. However, the greater question for a devout Evangelical is whether or not you believe that you fit into this category of person. It is one thing to believe that the Father wants to minister to, or pour into, a broken soul at the end of their rope. It is another thing entirely to admit that you yourself are brokenhearted and in need of healing.

No doubt, many of you will read this and think, "But I really don't have need for healing. I've never been sexually abused. I've never lost a parent. I've never experienced trauma. I don't really have any baggage!" How do I know this? I know this because that was my story. I was raised in a God-fearing home, in a loving family, by parents who modeled what it looks like to live by faith. What baggage could I possibly bring to the table?

As the Lord began peeling back the layers of my "self," the person who I thought I was, He started revealing more and more areas of wounding that He wanted to heal. A wound does not have to mean trauma. A wound does not even have to mean pain. But, we do have wounds, and they do need healing, as they usually inhibit our ability to experience, hear, or be ministered to by our Heavenly Father through His Spirit.

This is a critical truth for us to understand! Evangelicals tend to attribute a lot of power to sin, and completely minimize the significance of wounds, or to use Bible terminology, brokenheartedness. Yet, the lies and perspectives of our broken hearts often are the impetus, or the catalyst, for our sin. They are often the root beneath habitual sin. As such, we will not be able to muster enough resolve to stop repetitive sinning on our own. We must receive healing from the Comforter.

The Holy Spirit as the Helper

"But the Helper, the Holy Spirit, whom the Father will send in My name, He will teach you all things, and bring to your remembrance all that I said to you." John 14:26

When we are told to "abide in Him…" in John 15, I believe this is a primary way we do so. Abiding in Him is to live in a perpetual state of listening for and submitting to the direction of the Holy Spirit. Here are some ways that the Spirit is our daily Helper:

Directs
"Then was Jesus led up of the Spirit into the wilderness to be tempted of the devil." Matthew 4:1

"And he came in the Spirit into the temple; and when the parents brought in the child Jesus, to carry out for Him the custom of the Law…" Luke 2:27

"So, being sent out by the Holy Spirit, they went down to Seleucia and from there they sailed to Cyprus." Acts 13:4

"…He had by the Holy Spirit given orders to the apostles whom He had chosen." Acts 1:2

Forbids
"They passed through the Phrygian and Galatian region, having been forbidden by the Holy Spirit to speak the word in Asia…" Acts 16:6

Moves/inspires
"…for no prophecy was ever made by an act of human will, but men moved by the Holy Spirit spoke from God." 2 Peter 1:21

Speaks through
"When they arrest you and hand you over, do not worry beforehand about what you are to say, but say whatever is given you in that hour; for it is not you who speak, but it is the Holy Spirit." Mark 13:11

"…for the Holy Spirit will teach you in that very hour what you ought to say." Luke 12:12

Relying the Holy Spirit as our Helper presumes that we are actually listening to Him, doesn't it? How will we understand His directing or forbidding us if not through our active listening for His voice? How will He speak through us or inspire us if we deny He even behaves this way?

The Holy Spirit as the Spirit of our Father

"For it is not you who speaks, but it is the Spirit of your Father who speaks in you." Matthew 10:20

The Spirit of our Father works for the express purpose of bringing us, His children, to Him. Unfortunately, many of us take the viewpoint that the Father was obligated to adopt us because Jesus died for our sins. We believe we have a Father in heaven, but the sort of disinterested dad that has much better things to do than to babysit us. The very truth of the matter is quite to the contrary; Our Father absolutely, genuinely, completely wants us. We are reminded throughout Ephesians of His kind affection toward us. Our Father wants to be with His children: Us.

Knits our hearts to the Father
"Because you are sons, God has sent forth the Spirit of His Son into our hearts, crying, 'Abba! Father!'" Galatians 4:6

Unites us in fellowship before the Father
"…for through Him we both have our access in one Spirit to the Father." Ephesians 2:18

Helps us pray to the Father
"In the same way the Spirit also helps our weakness; for we do not know how to pray as we should, but the Spirit Himself intercedes for us with groanings too deep for words; And He who searches the hearts knows what the mind of the Spirit is, because He intercedes for the saints according to the will of God." Romans 8:26, 27

Facilitates prayer
"But you, beloved, building yourselves up on your most holy faith, praying in the Holy Spirit…" Jude 1:20

Pours God's love into our hearts
"…and hope does not disappoint, because the love of God has been poured out within our hearts through the Holy Spirit who was given to us." Romans 5:5

Our Father wants to pour into, or minister, to us. It is in this aspect of God's nature that He is most interested in caring for us, tending to our wounds, and whispering sweet-nothings into our ears. Now, because it is so foreign to us and impossible on our own behalf, our kind Father gives us a way to connect with Him; He gives us His Spirit. Imagine your own child, perhaps going away somewhere where it is impossible for her to be with you. As a way to keep the connection with her and to give her the love and affirmation she needs until she can be with you once again in person, you give her a cell phone. In a very small way, that cell phone is the role the Spirit of our Father plays in connecting our hearts with His.

The Holy Spirit as the Spirit of Promise

The Spirit of Promise is the mark of God upon His children that signifies His adoption of our frail hearts.

Is a Seal
"In Him, you also, after listening to the message of truth, the gospel of your salvation--having also believed, you were sealed in Him with the Holy Spirit of promise…" Ephesians 1:13

Is a Promise
"Therefore having been exalted to the right hand of God, and having received from the Father the promise of the Holy Spirit, He has poured forth this which you both see and hear." Acts 2:33

Is a Guarantee
"Now He who has prepared us for this very thing is God, who also has given us the Spirit as a guarantee." 2 Corinthians 5:5 NKJV

In the role of the Spirit of Promise, the Holy Spirit commemorates our adoption by the Father. He is the evidence of our sonship. The extent to which we allow Him to show Himself as this great evidence in our life will impact the level of effort we instinctively put into proving our salvation and accepting the worth our Father bestows upon us.

The Holy Spirit as the Spirit of Life

"For the law of the Spirit of life in Christ Jesus has set you free from the law of sin and of death." Romans 8:2

The Spirit of Life energizes and activates the work of the Father. He is the source of empowerment and ignition for the gifts in each believer as they are employed for God's purposes.

Comes upon
"And there was a man in Jerusalem whose name was Simeon; and this man was righteous and devout, looking for the consolation of Israel; and the Holy Spirit was upon him." Luke 2:25

"But you will receive power when the Holy Spirit has come upon you; and you shall be My witnesses both in Jerusalem, and in all Judea and Samaria, and even to the remotest part of the earth." Acts 1:8

"While Peter was still speaking these words, the Holy Spirit fell upon all those who were listening to the message." Acts 10:44

Baptism
"As for me, I baptize you with water for repentance, but He who is coming after me is mightier than I, and I am not fit to remove His sandals; He will baptize you with the Holy Spirit and fire." Matthew 3:11

"I baptized you with water; but He will baptize you with the Holy Spirit." Mark 1:8

Filling (before Pentecost)
"For he will be great in the sight of the Lord; and he will drink no wine or liquor, and he will be filled with the Holy Spirit while yet in his mother's womb." Luke 1:15

"And his father Zacharias was filled with the Holy Spirit, and prophesied, saying…" Luke 1:67

"When Elizabeth heard Mary's greeting, the baby leaped in her womb; and Elizabeth was filled with the Holy Spirit." Luke 1:41

Filling (at Pentecost)
"And they were all filled with the Holy Spirit and began to speak with other tongues, as the Spirit was giving them utterance." Acts 2:4

Filling (after Pentecost)
"And when they had prayed, the place where they had gathered together was shaken, and they were all filled with the Holy Spirit and began to speak the word of God with boldness." Acts 4:31

Some people define their belief or disbelief of the work of the Holy Spirit by what they think happened in Acts 2 when the Holy Spirit filled the first Christians after Jesus ascended. Some say that since the apostles spoke in tongues afterward, that we too must speak in tongues as a result of receiving the Holy Spirit. My challenge to these brothers and sisters is that in other cases, people who were filled with the Holy Spirit upon conversion did not speak in tongues, rather, they prophesied, or preached, or taught, or praised God. Tongues is not the Biblical norm when people are filled with the Spirit.

Others say that the events of Acts 2 were a one-time deal. The Holy Spirit descended on those people specially, once and for all. Therefore, we should not expect anything like that to remotely happen outside of that event. That moment, they say, was the ushering in of the Holy Spirit and the monumental event that would change the world forever. To these brothers and sisters I would say that this was not the first time these people received the Holy Spirit. In John 20:22, Jesus breathed on His disciples and told them, "Receive the Holy Spirit." Nor was this the first time that people had been filled with the Spirit. In Luke 1:67, Zacharias is filled with the Spirit, long before that monumental day of Pentecost. Finally, this was not the last time that events like those at Pentecost happened. In Acts 4:31, the Holy Spirit again shakes things up and fills people, inciting people to speak the word of God with boldness.

As a final note here, when we pre-define or deny the work of the Spirit of Life, it is exactly that life that we miss out on. I remember first-hand how dead I felt inside before the Spirit of Life was allowed to flourish. And I can also describe being in settings where a person was behaving as though the Holy Spirit was filling them, but the outcome was dead: dead works, dead performance, and dead theatrics.

The Holy Spirit as the Spirit of Grace

"I will pour out on the house of David and on the inhabitants of Jerusalem, the Spirit of grace and of supplication, so that they will look on Me whom they have pierced; and they will mourn for Him, as one mourns for an only son, and they will weep bitterly over Him like the bitter weeping over a firstborn." Zechariah 12:10

What we know from Zechariah is that the Spirit of Grace compels mankind toward an authentic connection with God. In ministering God's grace to us, He elicits a response of brokenness and yieldedness from His children.

Indwells
"Or do you not know that your body is a temple of the Holy Spirit who is in you, whom you have from God, and that you are not your own?" 1 Corinthians 6:19

"But if the Spirit of him that raised up Jesus from the dead dwells in you, He who raised Jesus from the dead will also give life to your mortal bodies through His Spirit who dwells in you." Romans 8:11

Restrains
"For the mystery of lawlessness is already at work; only He who now restrains will do so until He is taken out of the way." 2 Thessalonians 2:7

Can be partaken of
"For in the case of those who have once been enlightened and have tasted of the heavenly gift and have been made partakers of the Holy Spirit…" Hebrews 6:4

Is a Gift
"Peter said to them, 'Repent, and each of you be baptized in the name of Jesus Christ for the forgiveness of your sins; and you will receive the gift of the Holy Spirit.'" Acts 2:38

"All the circumcised believers who came with Peter were amazed, because the gift of the Holy Spirit had been poured out on the Gentiles also." Acts 10:45

As the Spirit of Grace, the Holy Spirit reveals to us the kindness of God, which is far greater than the evil of the world. Take in the words of Romans 2:4 as evidence, "Do you think lightly of the riches of His kindness and tolerance and patience, not knowing that the kindness of God leads you to repentance? Yes, the Holy Spirit convicts us of sin, but He also reveals the kind affections of our Father freely toward us.

The Holy Spirit as the Spirit of Holiness

"…Who was declared the Son of God with power by the resurrection from the dead, according to the Spirit of holiness, Jesus Christ our Lord…" Romans 1:4

The Spirit of Holiness affirms that Jesus Christ was who He said He was, the Son of God. He performs the transforming work of salvation:

Sanctifies
"…To be a minister of Christ Jesus to the Gentiles, ministering as a priest the gospel of God, so that my offering of the Gentiles may become acceptable, sanctified by the Holy Spirit." Romans 15:16

Regenerates
"However, you are not in the flesh but in the Spirit, if indeed the Spirit of God dwells in you. But if anyone does not have the Spirit of Christ, he does not belong to Him. If Christ is in you, though the body is dead because of sin, yet the spirit is alive because of righteousness." Romans 8:9, 10

Cleanses
"...how much more will the blood of Christ, who through the eternal Spirit offered Himself without blemish to God, cleanse your conscience from dead works to serve the living God?" Hebrews 9:14

We have examined many different elements of the ministry of the Holy Spirit, and we have looked at them in the context of the different names the Bible gives Him. Now, the reality is that different passages of Scripture portray the Spirit of God uniquely for the point they are making. Passages that speak of reassurance portray the Holy Spirit as the Comforter. Passages that warn of heresy speak of the Holy Spirit as the Spirit of truth, and so on. However, the Holy Spirit does not segment or compartmentalize His activity in real life. He ministers comprehensively at all times, because the needs of our hearts are complicated and intertwined. His interaction with us is precise and deliberate.

The Holy Spirit as the Spirit of Truth

"But when He, the Spirit of truth, comes, He will guide you into all the truth; for He will not speak on His own initiative, but whatever He hears, He will speak; and He will disclose to you what is to come."

The Holy Spirit was active in this role throughout the Old Testament, through major prophets and minor, through moments of prophetic activity in people other than prophets, and finally, into the New Testament in the same capacity.

Reveals
"...Which in other generations was not made known to the sons of men, as it has now been revealed to His holy apostles and prophets in the Spirit..." Ephesians 3:5

"And it had been revealed to him by the Holy Spirit that he would not see death before he had seen the Lord's Christ." Luke 2:26

Testifies
"God also testifying with them, both by signs and wonders and by various miracles and by gifts of the Holy Spirit according to His own will." Hebrews 2:4

"...Except that the Holy Spirit solemnly testifies to me in every city, saying that bonds and afflictions await me." Acts 20:23

"The Spirit Himself bears witness with our spirit that we are children of

God..." Romans 8:16

Bears witness
"And we are witnesses of these things; and so is the Holy Spirit, whom God has given to those who obey Him." Acts 5:32

Guards truth
"Guard, through the Holy Spirit who dwells in us, the treasure which has been entrusted to you." 2 Timothy 1:14

Signifies
"The Holy Spirit is signifying(indicating) this, that the way into the holy place has not yet been disclosed while the outer tabernacle is still standing..." Hebrews 9:8

Teaches
"...For the Holy Spirit will teach you in that very hour what you ought to say." Luke 12:12

Identifies Spiritual roles
"...The Holy Spirit has made you overseers, to shepherd the church of God which He purchased with His own blood." Acts 20:28

Truth is a major operation of the Holy Spirit. In some cases it is direct, straightforward truth. In other cases it is metaphorical. Sometimes it is revelatory, confirming, or testifying, but it always represents the heart of God.

Interaction with the Holy Spirit

As we have seen, the Holy Spirit has many different roles and functions. The Spirit has an intellect and reason. The Spirit also has emotion, and as such, can be offended and quenched.

Can be quenched
"Do not quench the Spirit; do not despise prophetic utterances. But examine everything carefully; hold fast to that which is good; abstain from every form of evil." 1 Thessalonians 5:19-22

Can be grieved
"Do not grieve the Holy Spirit of God, by whom you were sealed for the day of redemption." Ephesians 4:30

Can be blasphemed
"Whoever speaks a word against the Son of Man, it shall be forgiven

him; but whoever speaks against the Holy Spirit, it shall not be forgiven him, either in this age or in the age to come." Matthew 12:32

"And everyone who speaks a word against the Son of Man, it will be forgiven him; but he who blasphemes against the Holy Spirit, it will not be forgiven him." Luke 12:10

Can be pleased
"it seemed good to the Holy Spirit and to us to lay upon you no greater burden than these essentials..." Acts 15:28

Can be lied to
"But Peter said, 'Ananias, why has Satan filled your heart to lie to the Holy Spirit and to keep back some of the price of the land?'" Acts 5:3

Can be requested
"If you then, being evil, know how to give good gifts to your children, how much more will your heavenly Father give the Holy Spirit to those who ask Him?" Luke 11:13

"...Who came down and prayed for them that they might receive the Holy Spirit." Acts 8:15

Can be resisted
"You men who are stiff-necked and uncircumcised in heart and ears are always resisting the Holy Spirit; you are doing just as your fathers did." Acts 7:51

Can be rejected
"So, he who rejects this is not rejecting man but the God who gives His Holy Spirit to you." 1 Thessalonians 4:8

Acknowledging our need for the Holy Spirit

Brothers and sisters, do we still have the Holy Spirit pigeonholed? After reading what the Scriptures describe as His role, His priorities, His activity and His passion, can we honestly say we understand the Holy Spirit? I don't know about you, but I get so inspired to learn more and more facets of God's persona, more and more attributes that defy understanding and labeling. The more I mature as His child, the more complex He becomes.

When it comes to the idea of being "Spirit-filled," do you still wince, having seen the spectacle that some people have made His work to be? Or, does your mind begin to swim, overwhelmed at His complex mastery of our everyday life? Can you really resist Him, or are you ready to experience God in a complete, well balanced, and representative manner?

So, how does this robust depiction of the Spirit of God have an effect in our hearts? I believe that it all begins with an acknowledgement in our hearts that we need the Holy Spirit. We need to be taught. We need to be comforted. We need to be healed. We need to be reconciled to our Father.

Acknowledgement begins the process of permission. You and I will never allow God to do what He wants within us if we refuse to recognize our need! Conversely, we do not want to spend years identifying our need without actually coming to Him to receive healing and comfort!

There is, no doubt, much confusion and misunderstanding about the way the Spirit of God operates. The Evangelical Church is undoubtedly leery of "going there" and pursuing a life that is abandoned to His filling. What we need to remember is that the Spirit is all about conforming us to the image of Jesus Christ,[40] who was yielded, empowered, and lived out *His* full destiny. Each time, and to each new degree *we* are filled with the Spirit, we are actually being released, bit by bit, into *our* full identity and full destiny. The moments may be brief, but they all point to longer and longer times of being filled with the Spirit, "until we all attain to...the measure of the stature which belongs to the fullness of Christ." Eph. 4:13

Is it any surprise that the enemy of our souls works to keep us fearful of the filling of the Spirit within us, and to delude some who mistakenly think they have it? The filling is directly related to our living out our destiny, one by one, for the Kingdom of Heaven. If he can keep an army of the sons of God from living out their roles, he has neutralized the entire army, without an offensive strike ever being launched against the powers of darkness.

We need to see God differently. We need to see the Spirit of God differently. We need to open up the box that we have so efficiently packaged Him in, and take Him out and allow Him to be exactly who He is for you and for me. And, we must not put restrictions on Him. We will surely quench His work when we do.

---

[40] Romans 8:29

Chapter 7

The Sevenfold Spirit of God vs. The Seven Abominations

"I realize now, as others affirm, that the more I experience the power of the Holy Spirit, the more evident it becomes that I truly cannot grasp His immensity."

The often misunderstood and underestimated Holy Spirit is described in Revelation as the "Seven Spirits of God," or the "Seven-fold Spirit" in today's jargon. This is a concept that is rarely presented in the Church today, probably because it is so hard to wrap our minds around it. It is briefly mentioned in only a few passages in Scripture, notably in Revelation 1:4, 4:5, 5:6, and also in Zechariah 4:10, where Zechariah uses the same terminology when he receives understanding about the symbolism of the Menorah, the candelabra symbolic of the Jewish faith.

Several years ago I was at a conference where one of the breakout sessions was entitled, "The Seven-fold Spirit of God." Needless to say, I was intrigued and I signed up for the session, eager to learn about this Biblical portrayal of the Holy Spirit. Unfortunately, the session was a waste of time. The speaker spoke in such generalities that it didn't illuminate the matter at all. In fact, it seemed more like a pep rally for the Holy Spirit, as the main takeaway seemed to be, "Isn't it awesome that the Seven-fold Spirit exists?"

The unanswered question lingered for many years, and as I studied and pondered it, the Scriptures began to reveal more and more pieces to the puzzle. In this chapter, we will look at each of these seven attributes in order to gain a fuller sense of the core nature of the Holy Spirit. What are the seven manifestations of the Spirit? We read the following description from Isaiah 11:2.

"The Spirit of the LORD will rest on Him, the spirit of wisdom and understanding, the spirit of counsel and strength, the spirit of knowledge and the fear of the LORD."

The Spirit of the LORD, the spirit of wisdom, the spirit of understanding, the spirit of counsel, the spirit of strength, the spirit of knowledge, and the spirit of the fear of the LORD. These are the seven natures of the Spirit of God. As the Holy Spirit ministers and operates in humankind, the balance of these emphases collectively represent the Father in a balanced manner.

Knowing this, the enemy of our souls has a rebuttal to the seven priorities, or emphases, of the Holy Spirit. He has the seven abominations. In this chapter we are not examining a counterfeit, so much as we are examining characteristics of Satan that find their way into the Body of Christ, quenching the Holy Spirit:

"There are six things which the LORD hates, yes, seven which are an abomination to Him: Haughty eyes, a lying tongue, and hands that shed innocent blood, a heart that devises wicked plans, feet that run rapidly to evil, a false witness who utters lies, and one who spreads strife among brothers." Proverbs 6:16-19

As we examine this contrast between the Spirit of God and the unholy counterfeit, we embark on a new leg of our journey together. For you see, this is where we begin to illuminate how God's children can so easily be swept up into the counterfeit of the work of the Holy Spirit, all the while thinking that we are walking in the light. This should not come as any surprise, given the fact that our enemy works to distract and deceive us in the subtlest ways.

Here are the seven attributes of the Holy Spirit's character, listed alongside what we consider to be Satan's counterpart from Proverbs 6:

1. The Spirit of the Lord vs. Haughty eyes
2. The Spirit of Understanding vs. A heart that devises wicked plans
3. The Spirit of Wisdom vs. One who spreads strife among brothers
4. The Spirit of Counsel vs. A lying tongue
5. The Spirit of Might vs. Hands that shed innocent blood
6. The Spirit of Knowledge vs. A false witness who speaks lies
7. The Spirit of Fear of the Lord vs. Feet that are swift to run to evil

Let us now examine how these counterparts are used to oppose these seven attributes of the Holy Spirit's character.

Spirit of the Lord vs. Haughty eyes

The Spirit of the LORD is the core attribute of the seven natures of the Holy Spirit, and it represents the authority of God. God provided a metaphor of this reality in Exodus 25 where He described the design for the Menorah, the Jewish candelabra with seven candles. The center stem is the main post from which the other candles branch off. It is the place of dominance, and as Matthew Henry describes, it represents "the spirit of government, by which he should be every way fitted for that judgment which the Father has committed to him and *given him authority to execute...*"[41] Over and over again, Jesus' contemporaries were amazed at how much authority He exuded when He spoke and when He taught; "No one ever taught like this Man..."

We view "haughty eyes," or pride, as the dominant counter to the authority of God. When we look at major events throughout the Scriptures, the fall of man, the murder of Abel, the tower of Babel, David vs. Goliath, etc, we see pride as the driving attitude of sin. What was it that drove Satan to oppose God in the first place? It was pride. And if Isaiah 14:14 speaks symbolically of Satan, it summarizes perfectly with this statement, "I will ascend above the heights of the clouds; I will make myself like the Most High." The king of Babylon had similar aspirations, and in true form, God ended his campaign, just as he ended Satan's.

Spirit of Understanding vs. A heart that devises wicked plans

Ephesians 4 is such a powerful chapter, in my opinion. In our context, the chapter speaks into the relationship between understanding and wickedness when it challenges us to not allow our understanding to be darkened, as the result is a hard heart and a head-first pursuit of "every kind of impurity."

Understanding is our mode of thought; perhaps we could call it our "rationale." There is a direct correlation here between a clouding of our conscience and a rationalization of sin. As Ephesians 4:19-19 describes, people have become calloused, desensitized to wickedness and shame, and have chosen to embrace it with zeal, or "greediness," as it says here.

Spirit of Wisdom vs. One who spreads strife among brothers

The Scriptures have much to say about wisdom; it is the principal theme of the book of Proverbs. It speaks a great deal of what wisdom looks like, and what the opposite, foolishness, manifests itself as. "Through insolence comes nothing but strife, but wisdom is with those who receive counsel." Proverbs 13:10

Proverbs 10 tells us that wisdom turns away wrath humbly and softly. James 3 tells us that the gentleness of wisdom leads to good behavior, in contrast to bitter jealousy and selfish ambition. Those lacking in wisdom are contentious, slanderers, and are incorrigible. They bring strife to brothers.

---

[41] "Commentary on Isaiah," by Matthew Henry

The Holy Spirit brings increased wisdom to the person who is maturing in Christ Jesus. We know from James 1:5 that we can ask God, who loves to give wisdom generously to His children. Living and behaving wisely is an evidence of the work of the Holy Spirit in our lives.

Spirit of Counsel vs. A lying tongue

In Psalm 1, we are exhorted to not abide by the counsel of the ungodly. This is because they do not understand the things of the Spirit, as they do not have the Spirit in them.[42] The Holy Spirit works to unite and connect brothers and sisters, children of God, and to confirm a message of truth between them. Thus, we are to follow the counsel of other believers over the counsel of the world. However, the ultimate foundational standard is Scripture, and as we "test the spirits," we are even to test advice from fellow Christians against the Scriptures.

Finally, we need to be aware of any witness of the Spirit within us, speaking to a different direction than other believers are encouraging us. After all, Galatians 2 tells us of Barnabas being swayed incorrectly by Peter, requiring Paul to deliver godly counsel for correction's sake. Acts 21 describes how the New Testament church tried to talk Paul out of going to Jerusalem once it was clear that he would be arrested there. Paul, however, did not take this counsel of men, as the Holy Spirit had directed him to go. These are just a couple of examples of how counsel that opposes that of the Holy Spirit is deceiving, whether it is intentional or not.

Spirit of Might vs. Hands that shed innocent blood

Almighty God. It is a title that has sort of lost its punch these days. Almighty; it is a descriptor that denotes an all powerful identity. God is clearly capable of incredible feats and miracles, and He consistently demonstrated this throughout Scripture, both through His own acts and through His children.

God sometimes responds with force when He is disrespected, in a momentary release of His might. Remember when the Spirit of God would come upon Samson? In one instance he tore out of the ropes he was tied with and killed a thousand men in the might of God.[43] What

---

[42] 1 Corinthians 2:14

[43] Judges 15:14,15

about when the Spirit of God stirred in Jesus as He observed the moneychangers in the temple? He made a whip and chased the offenders out of His Father's house, destroying their booths and pouring out their money.[44] How about when Elijah made a spectacle out of the pagan prophets of Baal as he called on God to remind people that He was still the one true God by consuming his water-soaked altar with fire from heaven?[45] These are all examples of God demonstrating His might and His vengeance.

What about human vengeance? What more needs to be said about "Hands that shed innocent blood?" Murder is obviously a sin and a crime, but for those who think they are exempt of this offense, the Bible equates hatred with murder. "Everyone who hates his brother is a murderer; and you know that no murderer has eternal life abiding in him" 1 John 3:15.

Spirit of Knowledge vs. A false witness who speaks lies

We know that Spirit enabled knowledge is actually pinpointed truth. A word of knowledge unlocks the door to the heart of the matter. When someone receives a word of knowledge, they are receiving specific truth for a specific purpose. Often, the Spirit is illuminating something for the express purpose of bringing conviction, healing, etc.

False witnesses work to the opposite effect. They misrepresent the truth. They work to bring condemnation. Where the work of the Spirit is toward healing and liberation, the lies of false witnesses are enslaving and can lead to further bondage.

Spirit of Fear of the Lord vs. Feet that are swift to run to evil

What is fear of the Lord? It is embodied best, in my mind at least, by a passage we examine more than once in this book out of the first chapter of the book of Revelation. John describes his "reunion" with his savior, mentor, teacher and friend, Jesus; only this time, Jesus doesn't appear as the man, but rather, as the glorified and resurrected Omnipotent Jesus. John's response is telling, "When I saw Him, I fell at His feet like a dead man."[46]

---

[44] John 2:13-17

[45] Kings 18:38-40

[46] Revelation 1:17

John fainted at the terrible sight of Jesus, the Almighty, in light of His splendor and spectacle, finally revealed. John now had a balanced view of Jesus: grace and judgment, intimacy and separation; He was homely yet lovely, and comforting yet terrifying.

Fear of the Lord, I believe, comes with respecting the extremes of God's nature. Notice that we do not say, "understanding the extremes of God's nature," as He is so indescribable that our intellect, emotion and will combined could never make sense of His nature. Fear of the Lord is the awe that comes with understanding that He would be justified in quenching our breath at any moment, yet knowing that He wants us to climb up in His lap like the little children His disciples tried to send away.

Those that do not fear God are those that do not believe in their need for grace, their wretchedness, and the impending consequences that await. Those that do not fear God are quick to commit sin, even looking for opportunity to do so. The quest for pleasure is more powerful than their desire for God, if it even exists at all.

The Seven Abominations in the Church

Brothers and sisters in Jesus, the great opposing counterpart that Satan has employed to oppose the seven Spirits of God is not solely at work in the world; it is in the Church! How many instances do we personally know of involving pride, lies, hatred, wicked intent and wicked pursuits, false accusations and division within the Church? Friends, the Church is the center of the enemy's attack, and he is using all the weapons in his arsenal to target the children of God. We must not simply stand against the counterparts of the enemy, we must know the Spirit and His ministry, His nature and His agenda! We must not only resist the enemy, but more importantly, we must know the Father! After all, isn't this what John described as a difference between spiritual adolescents and spiritual fathers? "I have written to you, fathers, because you know Him who has been from the beginning. I have written to you, young men, because you are strong, and the word of God abides in you, and you have overcome the evil one." 1 John 2:14

- Haughty eyes, or Pride, is undoubtedly the biggest problem in the Church today. Our pride drives our motivations, our agendas and our perspectives. Pride is what leads to church splits. Pride is what inhibits the work of the Holy Spirit in the Body of Christ. Pride is exactly what the enemy wants to encourage because it will keep the Church from ever experiencing true authority in Christ.

- A heart that devises evil plans; doesn't that remind you of Judas? Judas was with Jesus for years, participating in miracles and likely even performing some himself! And yet, one of Jesus' closest friends began to devise wicked plans. Should we really be surprised that this happens in the Church today? We read of Sunday School teachers, preachers and missionaries that have not just "accidentally" found themselves in sin, they have crafted elaborate infrastructure to facilitate sin.

- One who spreads strife among the brothers-it happened in the early church, and it certainly happens today. Sometimes the contention is noble, and sometimes it is petty. Whatever the matter, we experience division in the Church today, just as in the case of Paul and Barnabas in Acts 15:37-40, where Barnabas wanted to take John Mark, and Paul refused as he was still upset that John Mark had deserted them previously. That contention was the end of Paul and Barnabas as a duo. Disagreements in the Church are divisive and distracting, and in my experience, at least one side ends up hurt and feeling misunderstood. Not surprisingly, many of these people leave the fellowship to search for unity elsewhere, and many wallow in their frustration, believing ultimately that God has let them down.

- A lying tongue. What shall we say of people in the Church that live a lie? Ananias and Sapphira lied to the rest of the Body and paid for it with their lives (Acts 5:1-11). It is interesting to consider that culturally, we accept lying as permissible, because while it is sinful, it is perceived as generally harmless, if not immature. God's perspective on the matter is apparently quite serious.

- Hands that shed innocent blood-"Everyone who hates his brother is a murderer; and you know that no murderer has eternal life abiding in him." Hatred is the direct counter to the work of the Holy Spirit in Ephesians 4, where we are told that He works to unify the Body and equip the saints. If we are harboring such ill will toward another brother, then it is to be assumed that we have not taken the matter to the Father and yielded it to Him. For you see, when we, like King David, present our feelings to God and await His ministering words, we receive healing. He doesn't take away the emotion we are struggling over, He instead changes our perspective on the subject and our emotions have no choice but to respond to His tender correction.

- A false witness that speaks lies fits very closely with the thing that God downright hated in the Old Testament; prophets that spoke of their own inspiration. There are countless examples throughout Scripture of men and women that prophesied, or spoke on God's behalf, using words that were constructs of their own motivations. In any case, they misrepresented God's heart, or His intent in certain cases, leading the people astray as a result. Anyone, and I mean anyone, that is in a position to represent God to the people, is under greater scrutiny and will be held accountable for their words! Desiree and I are certainly included in this statement! One of the most striking examples that I can personally recall is from a pastor that I used to sit under. I distinctly remember the day that he told the congregation, "If anyone ever tells you that God gave them a word for you, don't believe it! It is from the devil!" This man misrepresented God to an entire congregation and as a result, hearts were hardened to the voice and the working of the Holy Spirit.

- Feet that are swift to run to evil-If the Holy Spirit is active in the hearts of believers, then why is it that we can be so easily lured to sin? Why is it that we can know what would be pleasing to God, and run the completely opposite direction? It must be that we do not truly know God, that we do not take Him seriously, just like Ananias and Sapphira that were struck down dead in their sin.

These counters to the Seven-fold Spirit of God comprise the tactics of our enemy to corrupt the Bride of Christ. We must be watchful and wary to protect the virtue of His Bride so that we are not ashamed at His coming.

The Holy Spirit is our guarantee of eternal life (Ephesians 1:13,14). How can we be sure of our salvation? The Holy Spirit is intended to be our assurance. If we have no idea who the Spirit is, how can we know we are saved? To understand the Father's guarantee for me, I must understand the Spirit of God as fully as possible: His sanctifying work, the "good works" and the "calling" He created me for (Ephesians 2:10), and I must understand the work of the Holy Spirit who empowers and enables us in our roles and gifting.

The Spirit of God is not to be trifled with. He struck down Ananias and Sapphira, dead in their tracks. He is not beholden to us. We may request Him, but we cannot summon Him. We cannot add Him to our list of accomplishments and acquisitions.

Charles Finney preached on this tragic reality, about how our motive in asking for the Holy Spirit is often selfish, yet masked in a cloak of nobility. We might ask for Him to empower our sermons, but what is our motive? Is it glory? Is it church growth? Is it to make preparation easier? We may ask Him to help us study, yet perhaps it is only our laziness that is inspiring that request. His point is that when we ask for the Holy Spirit, we must accept His intervention on His terms exclusively.

> It is common for persons to resist the Spirit in the very steps He chooses to take. They would make the Spirit yield to them; He would have them yield to him. They think only of having their blessings come in the way of their own choosing; He is wiser and will do it in his own way or not at all. If they cannot accept of his way, there can be no agreement. Often when persons pray for the Spirit, they have in their minds certain things which they would dictate to him as to the manner and circumstances. Such ought to know that if they would have the Spirit, they must accept Him in his own way. Let him lead, and consider that your business is to follow. Thus it not infrequently happens that professed Christians maintain a perpetual resistance against the Holy Spirit, even while they are ostensibly praying for his presence and power. When he would fain draw them, they are thinking of dictating to him, and refuse to be led by him in his way. When they come really to understand what is implied in being filled with the Spirit, they draw back. It is more and different from what they had thought. That is not what they wanted.[47]

If we are to grow in the Spirit, we must yield over our agendas to Him, and let Him work in us and through us on His terms. When we are truly living in the fluidity of the Spirit, being led and empowered by Him, we are aligned with the Father. We are about our Father's business. This is the time, more than any time before, when the enemy of our souls will increase the opposition in our lives.

---

[47] Charles Finney, "On Prayer for the Holy Spirit," Lecture V, The Oberlin Evangelist, May 23, 1855

CHAPTER 8

AUTHENTIC VS. COUNTERFEIT: SPIRITUAL FRUIT

"I found myself questioning whether I actually experienced the fruit of the Spirit. I realized that since I had no concrete evidence of the real thing, I didn't know how to tell it apart from the fake."

We are told that Satan disguises himself as an angel of light.[48] Why would Satan need to do this? There would seem to be so many other effective ways to deceive the world. The key word here is infiltration. You see, if the devil can keep people distracted from the true and authentic, and occupied with the false and misleading, it would likely preclude that they would ever "wake up" from it, because they would assume they were in the will of God. In other words, if you think you are correct, especially if your "correctness" corresponds with the moral majority, then your feeling of justification is rock solid. To quote Matthew 6:23, "…if your eye is bad, your whole body will be full of darkness. If then the light that is in you is darkness, how great is the darkness!"

Being Content with Counterfeits

If the enemy can keep believers relatively well fed on counterfeits, then they probably won't realize what they are missing. I have personally experienced this. Coming out of my twenties, God began showing me aspect after aspect of my "spirituality" that was off target. God had to show me that the holiness I tried so hard to display was in fact, pretense. God spoke to me through Oswald Chamber's devotional reading for December 2 in *My Utmost for His Highest*. It is simply titled, "Christian Perfection." Two sentences nailed me. "The emphasis of holiness movements tends to be that God is producing specimens of holiness to put in His museum. If you accept this concept of personal holiness, your life's determined purpose will not be for God, but for what you call the evidence of God in your life." He nailed it!

I had been building evidence of Godliness. It wasn't actual Godliness-it was something that looked like it. If it were true Godliness, it would have been the result of communion with Him. But since I was becoming aware of the fact that I didn't truly know the Father, my Godliness didn't originate with Him. I was like the person in 2 Timothy 3 who has a form of godliness yet denied its power, always learning, yet never able to come

---

[48] 2 Corinthians 11:14

to the knowledge of the truth. Worse yet, I was trying to hold other people to my own standard!

I had become so correct in my own mind that it was nearly impossible to distinguish the difference between true godliness and the version I had concocted. But, it is like Jesus said to the Pharisees in John 5:39-40, "You search the Scriptures because you think that in them you have eternal life; it is these that testify about Me; yet you are unwilling to come to Me so that you may have life." Religious folks were scouring the Scriptures, yet completely missing the heart of God's message.

The dark side, the great charlatan, presents himself as an angel of light, a representation of good and morality, by mimicking the authentic, inspired work of the Holy Spirit. We need to be wary of the sophistication of these counterfeits. Equip yourselves, and take up your magnifying glass to examine the difference. Even now, the words of Jesus should wake us up to this need, "Behold, I send you forth as sheep in the midst of wolves: *be ye therefore wise as serpents*, and harmless as doves." Matthew 10:16

True vs. Counterfeit Spiritual Fruit

We begin our examination of truth vs. counterfeits in the area of spiritual fruit. Why here? We begin here because this is generally where the first results of salvation appear. The evidence of the Holy Spirit within us is: love, joy, peace, long-suffering, gentleness, goodness, faith, humility, and self-control.[49] It should be noted that as believers, these fruit are not automatic, they are not instantaneous. We must grow in them. The fruit must be cultivated within us.[50]

What purpose do the fruit of the Spirit hold in the Father's great design? We know that the Spirit restrains evil in the world,[51] and I believe He does so in part through God's children as we exhibit His fruit. We also know that, united with the Holy Spirit, we are God's temple on earth.[52] Furthermore, we are individually home to the Holy Spirit, who works in us to illuminate, teach, reveal,' and remind us of the truth of God's Word. We, in and of ourselves, are incapable of discerning and unmasking the

---

[49] Galatians 5:22,23

[50] 2 Thessalonians 3:5, 1 Timothy 6:11

[51] 2 Thessalonians 2:7

[52] Ephesians 2:19-22

counterfeits of the enemy. It is the Spirit of God within us that bears witness of the truth and illuminates the designs of the enemy.

The fruit of the Spirit have this effect because they are the attributes of God, and in some cases, as with the very first fruit, Love, it is His core identity; God *is* Love. The presence of God illuminates the dark wickedness of this fallen world, and He invites and allows us to be part of His process.

Love (of God) vs. Love (of self)

Love of God
The love of God is perfect, because it is a core, immutable attribute of a perfect God. Scripture is clear-if we do not love, we do not know God. Period. Why? Because God Himself *is* love.[53] We *know* that perfect love casts out fear,[54] but do we KNOW it? To experience even the smallest trace of God's perfect love toward us is to completely extinguish fear. We've heard that God is love our entire lives. It has been quoted by everyone: hippies, civil-rights leaders, Sunday School teachers and cultural Christians. How many of us have come to roll our eyes when we hear it quoted (or misquoted), as if its appropriation by popular culture has diminished its validity as inspired scripture?

Paul reminds us that the Love of God originates with Him pouring into us through the Holy Spirit.[55] Peter confirms that we must grow in the fruit of the Holy Spirit, and he says that in doing so, we become partakers of the very nature of God![56] Does that strike you as mind-blowing?! When we talk about the Love of God, we are not talking about some distant, cosmic love that God taps into to do amazing things for the human race. God doesn't have love, HE IS LOVE! Remember, He is the source, and these fruit are all just His attributes!

Romans 5:5 reminds us that God's love has been poured out into us! We are now partakers of His divine nature! The same love that He loved the world with to give His only begotten Son, that whoever should believe in Him would have everlasting life, this same love is the love that is poured into us. This is the same love we love others with. What are the

---

[53] 1 John 4:8

[54] 1 John 4:18

[55] Romans 5:5

[56] 2 Peter 1:3-9

implications here? We don't have a knock-off of His love, a diluted "human" version watered down especially for our pint-sized hearts. We don't have the "trial" size. We have the full version.

I know what you're probably thinking; "Yeah, right. I have been a Christian for years and I know I don't have His amazing love overflowing out of my heart." Why is that? It may be that you haven't considered that it is possible. Maybe it is because you are still growing! Paul indicates that one of the reasons God instituted the roles for the Body of Christ is to continually grow the members, you and me, until we match the fullness of Jesus Himself.[57]

What is the good news? God is nowhere near completing His good work in me. I am in progress, and so are you.

Love of Self
Paul speaks of certain acquaintances who have left him unsupported, stating that, "They all seek after their own interests, not those of Christ Jesus."[58] When Jesus rebukes Peter, He chides him for not being mindful of the things of God, but rather the things of man.

A subtle counterfeit is the self-love that promotes the ability and worthiness of self outside of God's provided identity, purpose and passion. Again, we are talking about the Church, as Jesus talked about Pharisees in His day, who loved the praise of men rather than the praise of God. These men received their reward here on earth.

I "led worship" for many years at our church. I would play my guitar and lead people in song, and I would gauge my success by how "worshipful" people appeared. The more, the better, and I especially enjoyed it when people told me that it was a great session. What validation! True success! I took pleasure in the praise of men. I would now say that the true celebration of ministry is in knowing that God has invited us to join Him in His great work, that He has a special place and purpose for us, and that we would be unfulfilled doing anything else. The fact that there may be "success" or a "positive outcome" only serves as further fodder for our praise of the Father.

---

[57] Ephesians 4:11-13

[58] Philippians 2:21

Joy vs. Happiness

Janet Erskin Stuart wrote, "Joy is not the absence of suffering, but the presence of God." Happiness, by default, is based in *happenstance*. Our human happiness is triggered by positive happenings.

Too often in the Church do we hear these two terms, *joy* and *happiness*, interchanged and confused with each other. Happiness is rarely spoken of in the Scriptures, but the Apostle Paul, a man who experienced great physical affliction, wrote extensively on joy. Jesus Himself confirmed that we will endure trials, tribulation, persecution and suffering. Yet, joy often seems to go hand in hand with these difficult circumstances.

Joy

It seems, more often than not, that when the Bible speaks of joy, it is in the context of suffering, stretching, emptying, and yielding. At first glance, it may seem that we should respond in joy when we encounter such hardship. But it is hard to imagine mustering a cheer out of the frustration of such trials. However, even in reading the scripture below, the author seems to indicate that the joy is already present. In other words, joy is the perspective we have in spite of circumstance.[59] We do not need to muster it as a response. It's existence generates our response of itself. Experiencing joy does not mean that the pain isn't excruciating. Having joy does not mean that we have no need to cry out to God.

In fact, Jesus indicates that joy is the result of our joining with our Father in heaven. Perhaps no other passage in the Scriptures summarizes Jesus' perspective on joy like John 15 does. He speaks of abiding in Him, and as such, we remain in the Father. He tells us to bear much fruit, and isn't joy a fruit? He also promises that if we abide in Him, that anything we ask will be done. And, in the midst of His discourse, He offers this statement. "These things I have spoken to you so that My joy may be in you, and that your joy may be made full."

What are we to draw from this passage? In the context of joy, we see a very clear connection between how deeply we choose to abide and how much joy we have. Going back the quote we opened with, joy is our partaking of the presence of God. How else are we to experience lasting joy but through abiding?

---

[59] 1 Peter 1:6-9

Happiness

What is your pursuit: joy or happiness? Perhaps the Biblical authority on the pursuit of happiness is King Solomon himself. He indulged his desires at an incredible level. He pursued happiness with reckless abandon and chronicled the outcome for us in Ecclesiastes chapter 2. He writes of how he set up his surroundings for the specific purpose of providing himself pleasure. He experienced great laughter, altered states of sobriety, achievement, design, the beauty of nature, accumulation of wealth, immersion in music, and many, many women. In his words, he indulged himself in every pursuit that promised pleasure. But, after the temporary happiness of each pursuit faded, all he could do was summarize it all as vanity.

This is how self-medication rules the lives of so many Christians and robs them of the "true and genuine" that their heavenly Father has for them. What are self-medications? They are the "security blankets" we use when we need to feel happiness. Some are known vices, while others may appear pretty harmless. Do you use any of these pursuits to experience momentary happiness or pleasure: food, alcohol, drugs, spending money, hoarding, dieting, self-expression, pornography, etc?

One that appeared harmless in my life was my love of Pepsi. I didn't just like it, I loved it! I loved the way it tasted when it was perfectly chilled. I knew the best place in the refrigerator to store the cans so they would cool to the right temperature. I could explain to you why I liked the taste of Pepsi better than its competitors. And, there was nothing in the world quite like cracking open a cold one after a long day at work. I found a disproportionate amount of pleasure in this soft drink. That is about the time that God began making me aware of this strange relationship with my beverage, and He began to invite me to leave it behind for something better: Himself. It wasn't easy to give it up-I had made it a part of my life. Yet, as I yielded it up this source of momentary happiness to my Father, He began to show me more and more ways that He wanted to be my source of pleasure.

Peace vs. False Peace

The peace that comes through the Holy Spirit is not "World Peace." Jesus asserts this when He says in John 14, "My peace I give to you; not as the world gives..." It is not a general, pervasive peace that comes as a result of conflict resolution. In fact, His peace is quite the opposite. Just as the Messiah did not bring the earthly kingdom that fit human description, He did not bring peace that fits our description. Just look at the world the early Church was born into. It was persecuted and oppressed on all sides, and yet it flourished. In the midst of it, the work of the Holy Spirit flourished, which means that the Holy Spirit's peace flourished as well. The reality is that the advancement of the Kingdom of God, in any form, produces conflict in the world and reaction from the devil.

Peace
Peace in the midst of conflict is the Spirit's way. One could build the case that we must have conflict in order to receive His peace. If there is no conflict, what need do we have for His peace? In the absence of conflict, we experience relaxation, we take the deep breath. We do not bat an eye at the notion of His peace. So, is it any wonder that we, the Church, are constantly blessed with conflict? The Holy Spirit is engineering scenarios where we can receive His peace! So, just as Jesus promises in John 14, we do not have to be troubled. The fact that He even makes this statement implies that there most certainly is trouble; we just do not have to be fearful of it.

False Peace
So now, the counterfeit should be clear. False peace is what the world calls peace: a lack of conflict. Isn't that what the philosophers fashioned when they wrote of Utopia? Yet, every time that mankind has tried to force Utopia into existence, it has met with abysmal results. Think of the Third Reich, Communism, or the LRA (Lord's Resistance Army) in Uganda. These systems began with a vision of an idyllic future, free from conflict or oppression. Of course, the originators defined conflicts and its causes differently, but still, their notion of peace was a major objective. Yet, the destruction that came from these pursuits of peace is some of the worst the world has ever seen.

Long-suffering vs. Permissiveness

There is so much emphasis on tolerance in the world today, that it has become "black-hole" terminology; it sucks matter into itself. The term tolerance nowadays implies that a person must not only accept another point of view, but acknowledge that it may be correct as well. When we view the term long-suffering in the Scriptures, it is easy to read into it the same way. But, as we will see, long-suffering does not imply approval of sin.

Long-suffering
What does it mean to be long-suffering? To be long-suffering is to patiently endure insult or grievance. This attribute of God's nature is described beautifully in Romans 2:4 where we read that His long-suffering goodness leads us to repentance. It is amazing to consider, isn't it? His long-suffering actually inspires a rejection of sin! In the same

way, Paul exhorts Timothy to "Convince, rebuke, exhort, with all long-suffering and teaching." Clearly, this extreme patience is not an endorsement of sinful lifestyle, in fact, it leads to the transformation of it!

Permissiveness
The counterfeit of long-suffering is permissiveness; it is the allowance, or worse yet, endorsement, of things that are displeasing to God within the Church, His divine institution. Paul reminds us that he is not concerned about judging "outsiders," as they are God's jurisdiction. But, for those within the Church, we are to provide a "checks and balances." His final words of 1 Corinthians 5:1-13 are extremely emphatic, "Remove the wicked man from among yourselves." There is no room for permissiveness within the Body of Christ.

Gentleness vs. Passivity

There are a lot of misconceptions about gentleness. Gentleness, in my opinion, is entirely misunderstood today. Gentleness is equated with "niceness." What do I mean by niceness? I am talking about not "rocking the boat." I am talking about a constant image of being sugary sweet. I am talking about a portrayal of "Christian elegance," as though we should wear cardigan sweaters and slacks and shoes with tassels in order to better represent Jesus. Ugh. Niceness.

It is a counterfeit, a shadow of what gentleness truly is. Entire movements have sprung up to address the plague of "niceness" in the Church today. John Eldredge, Erwin McManus and others have illuminated this subject quite effectively through books, groups and rallies like the Wild at Heart boot-camp, and The Barbarian Way. Jesus was tough, His disciples were tough. They had to be. The men and women of the early church were strong; they had to be. They lived in a time of great oppression from every side, and Christianity was about to undergo a severe persecution from Rome. There was no room for general niceness. "Nice" would never have survived. Yet, this is a characteristic that has become praiseworthy in the Church over the years.

Gentleness
Gentleness speaks of a deliberate tenderness toward other people: gentle words, gentle embraces, and gentle reproof. Paul, in writing to the Thessalonians, refers to himself as a "nursing mother" who "tenderly cares for her children."[60] We have to remember the context of this gentleness though. He has just been beaten, yet continues to minister in

---

[60] 1 Thessalonians 2:7

boldness and authority. It is in his sweet affection that Paul reminds them that he doesn't patronize them with flattering speech, tickling their ears, so to speak. Just as any good parent does, he shows a balance of correction and encouragement, but it is all born out of the Spirit's gentle approach working through him.

Paul isn't the "nice" man we talked about earlier. He rocks the boat where necessary. He is not sugary sweet, even in his tenderness. He instead shows us many layers to his character: boldness, endurance, strength, humility, authority, and of course, gentleness.

Passivity

The general "niceness" that is sucking the life out of our souls is really passivity. It is a resignation and a reluctance to engage our passion. It is a hesitance to allow our emotions to manifest. It is a dismissal of our dreams. Maybe worst of all, it is an unwillingness to fight. As a result, we, the Church, have forgotten how to fight. When we think of the Church and fighting in the same breath, we instantly think of the Crusades. We have been told how oppressive the Church was, how power-hungry and corrupt the Knights Templar were, and that's where the story fades into infamy, to permanently take the fight out of the Church, once and for all.

Jesus stirs things up a bit with His words, "I have come to cast fire upon the earth; and how I wish it were already kindled! But I have a baptism to undergo, and how distressed I am until it is accomplished! Do you suppose that I came to grant peace on earth? I tell you, no, but rather division…" Luke 12:49,51

Men and women of faith, let me encourage you that there is most definitely a time for peace, yet more importantly, there is a time for war. The important thing is to hear and respond to the Holy Spirit's invitations and promptings in your heart. He is the one that illuminates the battles that need to be fought, as well as the moments that call for gentleness and tenderness.

Goodness vs. Situational Morality

Goodness is generally defined as virtue, excellence or integrity. Integrity is commonly described as how you behave when no one is watching. In Job 1:8, God calls Job "a blameless and upright man…" Job understood the concept.

Goodness

When we think of goodness, or integrity, in the Bible, who do we think of first? Joseph is the person that comes to my mind. I think of the continual advances that Potiphar's wife made on Joseph, becoming increasingly adamant and literal in her pursuit of him. We all remember the story, don't we? The day she finally made her move on him, Joseph ran from her and fled this opportunity to sin.[61]

Joseph did not fall to temptation. In an age when notable figures fall from grace quite frequently, it seems almost baffling to consider how Joseph maintained his purity in this extreme situation. One could argue that his integrity was not based in an academic faith, but rather in deep experience of the rescue and provision of Jehovah Jireh Himself.

Situational Morality
What is situational morality? It is the use of a double standard. It is, in some cases, represented by our ability to engage in willful sin on Tuesday, and then hold a brother or sister to a Pharisaical standard on Wednesday. In any case, situational morality is a dead-giveaway of an academic Christianity. It is a symptom, most often, of a life that has not been transformed by the work of the Holy Spirit.

Here is an example from my own life. I remember, at 17 years of age, being one of "those" Christians. I relentlessly held people to the highest standards, and was judgmental when they did not measure up. I was in constant service at church, and participated in short term mission trips every year. I even invented ways of being more spiritual; I promised God that I would never taste alcohol. I was pretty confident in my image as a follower of Christ. Yet, I had my own sins that I just sort of "factored in" to my life. I even remember a moment when a friend of mine was telling us a story of a recent sexual encounter he'd had. As I sat there listening, I was jealous of him. I actually wondered why he was so "lucky." I wanted what he had experienced.

Now, if you had asked me pointedly, "Brandon, is sex outside of marriage acceptable?" my answer would have been an emphatic, "NO." But, the reality was that I was operating in a mental belief system called Christianity, not a radical, powerful, authoritative, life-altering encounter with God. You see, when all you have is a mental belief system, then arguments can persuade you. Sure, they can be actual human arguments, but most often, they are subtle arguments that the enemy brings in, under the radar. We are often swayed in these scenarios because we are so hungry for vitality, excitement, fulfillment, adventure, and a need to feel alive, that we readily accept the counterfeit the enemy offers, instead of the authentic original that God has waiting for us.

---

[61] Genesis 39

Yet, because we are such paradoxes in this mindset, we can easily step out of such a scenario and turn right around to point the finger at someone else. It is for this reason that Jesus tells us to take the log out of our own eye before trying to take the speck out of our brother's eye.[62]

Faith vs. False Faith

We will return again to the topic of faith when we look into spiritual gifts. Here, however, faith is a result of the work of the Holy Spirit, different and unique from the spiritual gift of faith.

Faith (in God)
So, what does faith look like as a result of growth and maturity in the life of a believer? "Now faith is the substance of things hoped for, the evidence of things unseen" Hebrews 11:1. Faith is always accompanied by hope, as hope is a sign of faith.

We certainly cannot effectively trust God for provision and not have any hope that He will provide, now can we? Faith is believing that God will fulfill His promise, any one of His promises, because He is our Father of Lights, and He loves to give us "good and perfect gifts" James 1:17.

False Faith
I once heard a quote, "Be sure to not assume that open doors are from God." The idea of entering open doors, doors of opportunity, is well engrained in the Church today. We even pray this way, that God would close doors to the wrong options and open the one door that will lead us into His plans, purpose or will. I certainly believe that God does use this approach quite often, but it is always on His terms. The hazard comes, in my opinion, when we start dictating the rules of engagement to God, as though we can set parameters for Him to operate within. "God, if the door closes, I'll know You said, 'No,' and if it stays open, I'll know that You want me to proceed." What if there are more than those two options?

I think we do this because it takes the risk out of listening for God's leading. It takes true faith to hear His voice and obey, to take action on it. By holding God to an "open door" model exclusively, we are trying to put the ball in His court. We are really trying to force Him to take the action, therefore allowing ourselves the comfort of just "happening" into His open door, as though His will is inevitable, and all we have to do is pray

---

[62] Luke 6:41

that the door at the end of our moving sidewalk stays open as we are carried toward it.

Friends, if we haven't figured this out by now, He doesn't operate this way very often, does He? God consistently interweaves the successes and failures, the plenty and need, the zeal and the apathy of our lives to create the beautiful tapestry that each one of us is as His children, as His new creations.

There is a second aspect to false faith. Many who profess a faith in Jesus Christ nowadays are practitioners of positive thinking. It seems so similar to faith, doesn't it? Both require an expectation of a yet unseen outcome, and both require a hope for the desired effect. There is, however, one major difference; positive thinking is based entirely on *us,* while faith is based entirely on God. Proponents of this false faith are banking on two things: the power of positivity, and the power of thought. What about the power of God?

Positive thinking is beneficial in certain aspects of life, but so are goal-setting, a "stiff upper lip" and "stick-to-it-iveness." These are all human inventions that are based in our ability to effect a situation. Let us not, for a single second, deceive ourselves into thinking that we can play God through our intellect. After all, isn't that dangerously similar to what Satan did before being stripped of his heavenly appointment?

Positivity is about numbing what we are truly feeling inside, all in the name of being a "good Christian." We commonly silence our fear, our doubt and our anxiety, by covering them with a thick layer of smiles and feigned cheerfulness. True faith, however, still allows for emotional honesty, as we pour out our hearts to our Father through the Holy Spirit within us who already knows what we are feeling. True faith occurs when we are emotionally honest with the Holy Spirit, yet still respond to His invitations to action.

Humility vs. False Humility

Jesus told a parable to some people who trusted in themselves that they were righteous, and viewed others with contempt. He told them about two men who went to pray: one was a religious leader and one was a tax collector. Most of us probably remember how the story goes. The Pharisee stands up and reminds God of all the ways he is spiritual and blameless. The tax collector, however, can't even lift his eyes to heaven, crushed under the weight of his great need for God's mercy.[63]

He addressed this parable to the self-righteous and judgmental. Friends, it is with great concern that I highlight this point. We are one of the most arrogant and judgmental groups of people on the face of this planet. Why do I say this? We behave this way because we know, without a shadow of doubt, that our belief is the right one. We believe entirely that we are on that narrow road that leads to eternal life. Tragically, we are often perceived as walking around with an air of self-righteousness about us. Jesus' point was striking; it was not the self-justifying religious leader that was approved before God, it was the humble man.

We often come across to each other and to unbelievers as though we are "better" than them. They call this a "holier-than-thou" attitude, and we come across as though we have nothing to improve on-that we couldn't possibly learn from an unbeliever. We forget that we are not very far removed from where they stand. As Paul reminds us, if it weren't for God's wonderful grace, we would still be in the same condition as them.

Humility
For the ultimate example of humility, let us look at Jesus Christ. We are challenged in Philippians 2 to hold the same perspective that Jesus did, as He set aside His power and privilege, and became empty for us.

How can we choose humility? What does it look like for a human to follow Jesus's example? If Jesus put Himself completely at the disposal of His Father in Heaven, then we can too. Jesus constantly checked in with the Father, inquiring of His Father's will, and consistently chose to fulfill His Father's business. And, Jesus was emphatic that His Father get all the credit.

We are invited to do the same. We are invited to abide with our Father-that state of connectedness and being together through the moments of the day. We are invited to join Him where He is at work. We are invited to yield ourselves to Him.When we make our existence all about joining Him in His business, we are pursuing active humility.

For the Christian, humility is the ability to act boldly in the authority of the Holy Spirit without taking any of the credit, glory or accolade. The Greek word for "to humble" is *tapeinoo*, and, as you would imagine, it has to do primarily with the lowering, abasing, and relegating of one's self. If true

---

[63] Luke 18:9-14

humility has everything to do with emptying ourselves of our own agendas and instead aligning with the Father's, doesn't it stand to reason that the process of active humility requires that we hear His voice so we can join Him where He leads and empowers? Isn't the opposite true then as well? One could build the argument that unless a Christian hears the voice of God and joins Him in His business, that person cannot experience true humility. True, active humility is dependent upon us knowing ourselves so we can submit our plans and perspectives to the Father's.

False Humility
If true humility has to do with emptying our "self" and aligning with the Father, how can we do this if we do not know our true self? If you are still living in the "false self," the "you" that has developed from all your life experiences, hurts, baggage, lies, vows, facades and barriers, then any attempt at humility would be directed towards a false identity. In simple math:

Suppression + False self = False Humility.

We see an example in the life of Moses. God has called him to lead the Israelites out of slavery in Egypt. God has made His agenda known to Moses, and He is revealing Moses' role in His business. Moses responds in a manner that, on the surface, may appear humble to most. He denigrates himself in response to God. Moses reveals that he is a poor speaker and may not be very "quick on his feet" when it comes to verbalizing thought. This sounds humble, doesn't it? Isn't this what society elevates nowadays as modest: when we don't think too highly of ourselves?

Moses's "humility" is really just a big excuse. Take note that he doesn't express his emotions to God in this situation. He doesn't follow up his objection with a final statement of submission to God. He just tries to get himself out of God's business with his false humility. Don't we all do the same thing in our own way? God doesn't accept Moses's "humble" view of himself.[64] Continuing through the story, God reasserts to him that He will be with his mouth. God kept bringing Moses back to the point, and back to His purpose. God was taking the focus off of Moses and putting it on Himself. False Humility is all about our view of ourselves. True Humility is all about our acceptance of God's view of us.

What are the implications for us today? If God didn't accept Moses's view of himself, does He accept your view of yourself? What excuses have

---

[64] Exodus 4:10-14

you come up with in the name of humility? How have you kept God at arm's length because you think it is better to have a low opinion of your physical condition, your created state, or your station in life? If it didn't excuse Moses from accepting his God-designed role and destiny, it certainly does not excuse you or me either.

Self Control vs. Asceticism

As we examine the fruit of the Spirit, we see a development of attributes that are the outcome and evidence of the Spirit's activity in our intellect, emotions and will. These attitudes are not attitudes that we could generate on our own. The versions that we *could* generate of our own resolve are the *false* versions.

This final fruit, self-control, is no different. It is an attitude or state of being that the Spirit of God generates. As such, it is not our self manipulation, coercion and confinement that is evidence of the Spirit's activity in our life. There are many lost people that are more self-controlled than Christians, if this is the barometer we are using for measurement. Instead, self-control must remain the fruit, the outcome of the Spirit's presence and permission in our whole self. The control of self, or the suppression of our own agendas and perspectives, happens as a result of what only the Spirit of God can do when we yield ourselves to Him. And, as is typical of the activity of the Spirit, there is absolutely nothing we can boast in, because it is not our action, our doing, that has generated the fruit. It is all Him, finally able to be Himself in me, after I have stepped out of the way. John the Baptist summed it up perfectly, "He must increase, but I must decrease." John 3:30

Self Control
For the immature believer, self-control begins as "sin-management," the mode of operation where life and accountability is structured by the rules we put in place to avoid sin. Life in this mode is very black and white. It is wrong to do _____, it is right to not do it. As we grow more and more into maturity, however, the black and white nature of this transactional living becomes frustrating and limiting. We start moving past sin management into "discipline," which in our vernacular tends to be interpreted as "being deliberate about something that requires effort." This could include deeper study of the Bible, reading through the Bible in a year, scripture memorization, waking up earlier to be with the Lord, more focused prayer times, etc. Finally, I believe that in maturity, self-control becomes most esoteric. It centers more on remaining "emptied of ourselves," having times of solitude with God, listening to His voice, and meditating on Him. Where do you find yourself in this process?

Asceticism

Asceticism is essentially a harsh version of self-control, or an extreme form of abstinence. You might think of it as a practice of self-denial for the sake of gaining God's favor through our sacrifice. This begs the question, "When we sacrifice things to God, why do we do so?" Is it because we find spiritual value in the fact that we have given something up? We must be cautious in this area. If Jesus Christ truly paid for our trespasses on the cross, then certainly, nothing we can "sacrifice" will please God. So, why would we ever fast? Why would we ever "leave father and mother" and follow Jesus? In the context of the grace and salvation of the New Testament, sacrifice or self-denial for denial's sake has little value. Instead, where it does impact our spiritual growth are the situations where the Holy Spirit nudges us, and prompts us to join Him in a specific way.

I recall a specific example a couple of years ago when I experienced this very typical working of the Spirit. I was praying for God to increase my awareness and experience of His Spirit. I had prayed for months about this need, when one day I clearly understood in my heart that I was to fast the next day. Wouldn't you know it; I immediately had to question the prompting. Was this really the Lord? Did He really want me to fast the next day? You see, the next day I was going to attend a Christian conference that is known to have a great breakfast and lunch. I finally submitted and accepted the Spirit's invitation to fast. The next day, I double-checked with the Lord, and yes, I was to fast through breakfast. I double-checked again at lunch, and yes, I was to continue fasting. I checked again at dinnertime, and he told me it was time to eat. Of course, I kept asking over and over again, just to be sure, but that was the end of it. I fasted on His terms, and I remember being perplexed that I had not experienced the immediate effect or value of the act. It was about two weeks later when God allowed me to experience more of the working of His Spirit. It was a profound experience that was ultimately related to the earlier invitation for me to fast. It was a deeply impactful experience with God that I am so grateful for, yet I have to wonder how many invitations I have not accepted from Him?

The important thing is to recognize when the Holy Spirit is calling us to join Him, and of course, join Him. If He calls us to fast, we should do so. But, to do it of our own initiative may not hold the results we are after. God challenges His people in Zechariah 7, asking them why they fasted and mourned. The question is whether we do so for our own justification, or whether we are doing it out of a loving response to the prompting of the Holy Spirit within us.

Chapter 9

Authentic vs. Counterfeit: Spiritual roles

"I didn't want to miss out on God's intent and His empowerment. I was not content with being a shadow of His design, I wanted the whole thing. I wanted all of it."

God designed a forum for His children to be empowered, encouraged, and edified; He designed and breathed life (the Holy Spirit) into the Body of Christ: the Church. The Greek word in the New Testament is "ecclesia," which means the "called-out ones." William Tyndale originally translated this word as "congregation," referring to the nature of the Body of Christ as a community of His people. By the time subsequent versions were available to the public, however, the wording had been "updated" to reflect where society was at; the word "church" had been substituted, perhaps in deference to the state-church that dominated religion of that time. The true meaning of this word, ecclesia, referred to a group of people that were called out for a specific purpose. What were we called out of? We were called "out of darkness and into His marvelous light."[65] What were we called for? We were called "...with a holy calling... according to His own purpose."[66] So then, the "church," or ecclesia, is simply a group of people called out of darkness and into His truth for His purpose. How then are we to function as this ecclesia?

He gave us instructions for the function of the "called-out" throughout the New Testament, but Ephesians 4 speaks specifically of certain roles He created, not solely for the administrative staff of the Church, but for every single member of His "called-out" to occupy for the express purpose of bringing pure attention and glory to Himself. "But to each one of us grace was given according to the measure of Christ's gift...He who descended is Himself also He who ascended far above all the heavens, so that He might fill all things. And He gave some as apostles, and some as prophets, and some as evangelists, and some as pastors and teachers, for the equipping of the saints for the work of service, to the building up of the body of Christ..." Ephesians 4:7,10-12

So, in keeping with Satan's strategy to oppose all things Godly, he has counterfeits for the roles that God intended His children to live out. Each of these false offices is designed for one thing; to deceive. From signs

---

[65] 1 Peter 2:9

[66] 2 Timothy 1:9

and wonders to misleading information, it is all intended to dazzle and preoccupy. Misleading information includes "partial truths." Partial truths are concepts that contain an element of truth, but are incomplete. Partial truths are often what the enemy uses to hammer Christians into ineffectiveness. Here's a biblical truth that gets exploited in this manner, "I am a sinner." I know many people that are paralyzed by self-doubt because they live in the belief that they are worthless and unusable by God. Sure, we were all sinners to start with. However, that is very, very limited information and only reflects one small part of the salvation story! The other part of this picture is that if we have been born-again, then we have been adopted by The Father, and we are now joint heirs with Jesus! As such, He has given us a token of our adoption, a guarantee, and it is the Holy Spirit in our hearts. The Holy Spirit works within us in many ways, but one way is to activate the gifts that He has given us in order to facilitate His good purpose for our lives. That good purpose is directly connected to our spiritual roles.

It is also through this Spirit that we are able to discern between the fakes and the real thing. In and of ourselves, we have no capacity to distinguish these matters. It is the Spirit of God within us that illuminates the darkness. It is the Holy Spirit who bears witness, testifies, of Jesus. It is this same Spirit that is grieved and quenched, in this context, by the misrepresentation of God. The Spirit of God cannot and will not tolerate our fleshly agendas in His name.

What kind of witness do we get from the Spirit when a counterfeit is at work? It is a warning within our hearts, a deep unsettled sense that something is not right. It is sometimes a very creepy feeling that makes us want to leave the setting or even to set things right. How many times have you felt this?

We have experienced this witness of the Spirit, this warning, in conservative settings as well as charismatic, in public meetings and in small prayer groups. It is always an experience that drives us to God in order to confirm what we have experienced. As 1 Thessalonians 5:21 exhorts us, "Test all things; hold fast what is good."

The enemy will do anything necessary to keep us blinded to our true identities, the roles we were created for. He will work to cheapen and dilute the significance of these roles. He will supplant authentic representations and will promote false examples of these roles. For the sake of our discussion, false examples are not opposites-opposites would be far too obvious. We are instead talking about counterfeits. Counterfeits are designed to distract and deceive the Church first, and the world second.

Apostle vs. False apostle

According to scripture, it appears that some people want the "glory" of being an apostle on the leading edge of the Church, even performing signs, wonders and miracles. The irony, of course, is that true authority in Christ comes with an emptying of self, a surrender to the will of God. Those who look for personal glory instead of giving all the glory to God may find themselves empowered by some force other than the Holy Spirit. Sure, it will be a close facsimile, but self-service and vainglory should be a dead giveaway to the discerning heart.

Apostle

Many people these days equate church planters and missionaries with apostles, as their function is about establishing the Church around the world, and that often times, God performs signs and wonders through them or their ministry to that end. Other people just claim that there are no modern day apostles; that the role was no longer needed once the Church was established. Some folks argue that the apostles couldn't exist today, because by default, they were the 12 disciples that walked with Jesus and were commissioned directly by Him. I do not believe this to be true. What about the apostle Paul? What about Matthias, who was voted in to replace Judas? What about Silas, Barnabas, Stephen and Timothy? They didn't walk with Jesus. How were they commissioned? I believe that God's design for the Church has not changed just because "the times" have.

The word "apostle" first appears in Matthew 10:2 with the statement, "Now the names of the twelve apostles are these: The first, Simon, who is called Peter, and Andrew his brother; and James the son of Zebedee, and John his brother; Philip and Bartholomew; Thomas and Matthew the tax collector; James the son of Alphaeus, and Thaddaeus; Simon the Zealot, and Judas Iscariot, the one who betrayed Him." Why was Judas included in this list if apostles are only the people that first established the Church after Jesus' ascension? If we include Judas, who interacted with Jesus first-hand, we must include other contemporaries who also interacted with Jesus, yet were not part of the 12 disciples. We are, of course, talking about the apostle Paul.

No doubt as a response to skeptics, Paul asserts to the Corinthians that he too is an apostle, as evidenced by his actions:

"The signs of a true apostle were performed among you with all perseverance, by signs and wonders and miracles." 2 Corinthians 12:12

Are you an apostle? The Biblical model shows apostles advancing the

Kingdom of God, often through signs and wonders. People are healed, demons are cast out, and God is glorified. And no particular denomination can take credit for it. God moves as He sees fit.

False Apostle
If the authority of an apostle is rooted in the emptying of selfish agenda, it may rightly be said that a false apostle is full of selfish agenda. Paul confirms this when he says, "But what I am doing I will continue to do, so that I may cut off opportunity from those who desire an opportunity to be regarded just as we are in the matter about which they are boasting. For such men are false apostles, deceitful workers, disguising themselves as apostles of Christ." 2 Corinthians 11:12-13

How interesting is it in Matthew 7:21-23 that Jesus addresses this very issue, before the position of Apostle was even identified. Of course, this applies to more than just Apostles:

"Not everyone who says to Me, 'Lord, Lord,' will enter the kingdom of heaven, but he who does the will of My Father who is in heaven will enter. Many will say to Me on that day, 'Lord, Lord, did we not prophesy in Your name, and in Your name cast out demons, and in Your name perform many miracles?' And then I will declare to them, 'I never knew you; DEPART FROM ME, YOU WHO PRACTICE LAWLESSNESS.'"

True, authentic empowerment by the Holy Spirit requires our yieldedness to Him. Those who mimic the role of an apostle without the genuine fueling of the Spirit of God do so with a desire for glory, a sure way to squelch His divine agenda.

Prophet vs. False prophet

God instituted the role of prophet in the Old Testament, and retained its function throughout the New Testament. Who is a prophet? In the Old Testament, we see examples of prophets like Samuel who occupied a central role in Jewish history. They advised kings and provided sort of a checks-and-balances to the crown as it ruled God's people. However, there were other prophets, like Amos. Amos was a shepherd. He was nobody special. He was a regular guy that God selected to be His mouthpiece for a specific purpose, to a specific people, and for a specific season. By the time of the New Testament, the major prophets were no longer present. The Jews were under foreign rule and they had no king of their own, and accordingly, there was no prophetic counterpart. God continued to reveal Himself to "minor" prophets, however, and Simeon and Anna are the first two we see in the New Testament in the book of

Luke, chapter 2. Prophets are regular folks, men and women, who God activates to deliver His Holy Spirit inspired message.

Prophet
Prophets are regular people who were built into God's design for the function of the Church. They are a stigmatized role in the Church, which is probably why Jesus Himself testified that "...a prophet has no honor in his own country" John 4:44. Do you remember that Jesus' own people wouldn't receive Him? They could not believe that the carpenter from Nazareth was a mouthpiece of Jehovah, let alone the Messiah. They viewed Him as self-righteous and high-and-mighty. Nowadays, when a person shares that they have a message from the Lord, how many of us instantly brace ourselves? How many of us instantly assume that the person is misguided, misinformed and mistaken? How many of us give them a patronizing gaze that reads, "This poor guy, he must not be very rooted in his faith." Finally, how many of us look at such a person with a level of contempt or disgust at their audacity to claim they have such a level of intimacy with the great Elohim Himself?

Is it any surprise that prophets are quiet in the conservative church? Is it disconcerting to know that they are active and engaged in their calling, but they have to live it out "under the radar?"

If it is the Holy Spirit that initiates and enables, then why are we such skeptics of the human being? Well, this should be obvious; we have too often seen people acting "on God's behalf" yet without the promised results, or worse yet, with divisive results. How often is this done by someone who is immature in the faith? So, what is the answer? I believe that we need better mentoring within the Body of Christ. I believe we are "the blind leading the blind," and that we need mature, seasoned Christians to model and train others in the proper use of these gifts and roles for the Church.

The Bible states that no true prophecy was ever made by an act of human will, rather, it was the Holy Spirit who gave the words.[67] Additionally, prophecy was not really about predicting the times and dates of future events. The Scriptures tell us that prophets who foretold the events surrounding the Messiah made "careful searches," diligently studying to put the pieces together to best understand what it all meant.[68] True prophets deliver the message the Holy Spirit inspires, simply put,

---

[67] Peter 1:21

[68] 1 Peter 1:10-12

and oftentimes rely on the rest of the Body of Christ to be inspired for the interpretation and application of it.

False prophet
A prophet can "minister" out of his or her own agenda, presuming on the nature or intent of the LORD. God takes this very seriously, as He is not one to be misrepresented without consequence. In Jeremiah 6 the prophets had placated God's children by promising them peace, but that was not on God's agenda, and there were consequences to pay. In Deuteronomy 18 God details the punishment for a prophet who spoke a word "presumptuously" in the name of the LORD.

Prophets, living and acting outside the will of God, have been known to become corrupt. Do you remember the story of Balaam from Numbers 22? Balaam was a prophet that was paid by Israel's enemy to curse God's people. Of course, God would have none of this, and He made sure that Balaam understood that Israel was to be blessed instead. Balaam, however, kept engaging with the enemy, trying to figure some other way to contrive a curse against Israel. God ultimately perplexed these efforts over and over until Balaam complied and blessed Israel before God and his enemies. Ezekiel 3 speaks of prophetesses who had false visions. Acts 13 speaks of a false prophet named Bar-Jesus. If it happened in the pages of Scripture, we can be sure that we are not exempt from this reality today.

In short, prophets are the mouthpieces of the Lord. Upon prompting by the Holy Spirit, they deliver truth from God, specific to a situation, season or service. Many people stigmatize this term and assume that it implies foretelling the future, as it often did in the Old Testament. However, the Lord speaks as He desires, when He desires, to whom He desires. As we discuss elsewhere in this book, He speaks to unbelievers, as well as those in sin. So, "hearing" from the Lord is not necessarily a measure of your maturity or spirituality.

Evangelist vs. False Evangelist

The word "evangelist" has become a parody in some circles, and quite unfortunately. When people speak of televangelists, they are often portrayed as excessive, theatrical, and greedy. What a tragedy! True evangelists are driven by a passion to bring as many souls as possible to the Father through Jesus Christ.

Evangelist

Of course, we are all called to make disciples throughout the earth, but some people just seem to have been born to be evangelists. You know what, they probably were!

I remember, many years before discovering my own unique identity as God designed me, that I felt guilty that I was not passionate for or effective at evangelism. I even went through our church's Discipleship/Evangelism training program. It was horrible. I was so far out of my element, yet other people seemed so at ease with it. It wasn't until I found my role in the Body of Christ that the "guilt" went away, and it wasn't until I began to recognize the voice of God in my heart that I could join His prompting to share the gospel where He had first laid the groundwork.

Philip is probably the first person we all think of when it comes to evangelists in the Scriptures. In Acts 8, we see a snapshot of his ministry. He went to where the need was and told people about the good news of Jesus Christ. The Holy Spirit harvested many, many souls into the Kingdom, and Philip baptized these people to commemorate what God was working among them.

Who do you know that fits this description? I can certainly think of people in our church who cannot "turn it off." Evangelizing is part of who they are-it is part of their identity, and as they move in tandem with the heart of God, He brings about a fruitfulness that could never be matched by a person pretending to occupy that role.

False Evangelist

"Some indeed preach Christ even of envy and strife; and some also of good will: The one preaches Christ of contention, not sincerely, supposing to add affliction to my bonds..." Philippians 1:15,16

"But though we, or an angel from heaven, preach any other gospel unto you than that which we have preached unto you, let him be accursed." Galatians 1:8

What is a false gospel, spread by false evangelists? Philippians 1 describes one type as a contentious, divisive message. Galatians 1 seems to refer to a different, more pleasurable message, designed to coddle the ears of men. Some call it a prosperity gospel, that God wants to make all your problems go away. Others say that God's financial blessing in your life is in direct proportion to your faith. The richer you get, the more faith you must have. How about this message? Jesus alone isn't enough to save you, you also need to _____.

It is very easy to deceive many people; just tell them what they want to hear! What differences do you see between Philip, the first "evangelist" mentioned by this title in the Bible, and false evangelists? Philip is all about Jesus. He is the singular motivation behind Philip's message. False evangelists, on the other hand, speak from their own perspectives and their own desires.

Pastor/Shepherd vs. False shepherd

The role of a pastor, or shepherd, in the Church is clear. If apostles and evangelists are for evangelism, then prophets, pastors and teachers are for discipleship. In other words, in the vernacular of Ephesians 4, they function for the unity of believers and the equipping of the saints. Nowadays, we tend to minimize the power and significance of this office, and many people even lump it in together with the role of "teacher." Obviously, in Western culture, pastors do have to teach, and teachers do have to shepherd, but we rarely see someone who excels at both.

Shepherd
Pastors are protectors and nurturers of the flock. If prophets are the cattle-drivers of the Church, pastors are the shepherds. Pastors are designed to vigorously defend the flock against anything that would divide the Church. Jesus Himself modeled this for His disciples and drove the message home when He told them, "I am the Good Shepherd," and "I have come that they may have life, and have it abundantly" John 10.

Shepherds of the day kept their sheep in a small pen, and they would sleep in the doorway, acting as a human barrier to any animal that tried to get in and harm the sheep. Accordingly, Jesus calls pastors to vigorously defend the flock. David recounts his own experience as a shepherd, fulfilling this task quite literally, foreshadowing the role that God would have him play over Israel's spiritual heritage:

"But David said to Saul, 'Your servant was tending his father's sheep. When a lion or a bear came and took a lamb from the flock, I went out after him and attacked him, and rescued it from his mouth; and when he rose up against me, I seized him by his beard and struck him and killed him. Your servant has killed both the lion and the bear; and this uncircumcised Philistine will be like one of them, since he has taunted the armies of the living God.' And David said, 'The LORD who delivered me from the paw of the lion and from the paw of the bear, He will deliver me from the hand of this Philistine.' And Saul said to David, 'Go, and may the LORD be with you.'" 1 Samuel 17:34-37

Ezekiel 34 speaks of God's anger when pastors/shepherds do not fulfill their duties. The shepherds He had placed over the Children of Israel "fed themselves" and did not feed His flock, they did not search for His sheep, and as a result, His flock became food for all the beasts of the field for lack of a shepherd.

This admonition from the Lord sets a clear tone for shepherds of the flock; protect His sheep, search out and minister to sheep that are hiding, anxious, etc., and feed His sheep.

False Shepherd
By definition then, false shepherds are those pastors that do not protect His sheep, do not seek out and minister to sheep that are hiding and hurting, and do not feed His sheep, or worse yet, leave the flock exposed or lead them personally into falsehood and unbiblical pursuits. Jeremiah 50 describes how false shepherds lead God's people aside, out of His resting places and into laborious, treacherous terrain.

My early childhood was spent in a home church that went tragically wrong. What started as a noble pursuit of God and community ended up as the power trip of a troubled man. The decline was so slow that it was hardly noticeable. It took years for the falsehood to be recognized. Ultimately, it was my parents who called the false shepherd out on the carpet and ended the charade once and for all, but unfortunately, the spiritual damage that this man left in his wake was devastating to many people. I continue to thank God for leading my parents in their confrontation, and I continue to pray for the friends who walked away from the God who had been so badly misrepresented to them.

I have seen firsthand the devastation a false shepherd can cause, and I do not take the warnings against them for granted.

Teacher vs. False teacher

The evangelical movement has something against it, from my vantage point. It has focused primarily on the teacher as its role of choice, and in certain unhealthy scenarios, the teacher has become so elevated that the extreme end result becomes a worship of knowledge, or Bibliolatry, as it has been sometimes called. Paul addresses a likely outcome in 1 Corinthians 8:1-3 when he addresses what people "knew" in a specific context: "Knowledge makes arrogant, but love edifies." He goes on to challenge the "high-and-mighty" when he tells them that they really don't know what they are talking about.

Knowledge is critical to our spiritual development. Hebrews 6:1 affirms the role that teaching plays in establishing a firm foundation for our growth in the Spirit. But, we must remember that it is only one ingredient, and teachers are only one of the essential roles that God designed for the function of the Body of Christ.

Teacher
Teachers expound on The Word and illuminate the message of the Bible. They provide instruction and foundational truth. They espouse theology and help keep the flock on course. Teachers help us "rightly divide the word of truth."

Teachers have a passion for making Scripture accessible and understood to God's people. The Holy Spirit is passionate about the same thing, and we know that the Spirit "teaches" us as part of His ministry in the Body of Christ. Furthermore, the Scriptures indicate that angels have been part of the teaching process as well. In Daniel 9, the angel Gabriel ministers to Daniel in several ways, one of which is instruction.

Instruction is critical to our establishment and rooting in the faith. The story that comes to mind right now is the passage in Acts 18:24-28 where we are introduced to the man, Apollos. According to the story, he was an eloquent man and "mighty" in the Scriptures. He had been taught well, and as passionate as he was, he taught openly about Jesus. The issue was that he only knew about Jesus through the teachings of John, and it seems that he was missing some key details, including the reality of the baptism with the Holy Spirit that Jesus Himself taught. Well, Priscilla and Aquila heard him teaching boldly in the synagogue, and they faithfully took him aside and "filled in the blanks," so to speak. This man and woman taught him the key details that he was missing about the message of Jesus Christ. Of course, the story only grows richer from here as Apollos ends up joining the disciples and becoming a powerful apologist for the gospel. Did you catch all the places in the story where instruction had occurred? This man was launched into his God-given destiny because of all the rich instruction he had received.

Teaching is especially critical when it comes to our understanding of the activity of the Holy Spirit. It is so easy for people to go off on tangents in this area. It is so easy for people to form theology out of a single scripture and therefore, misdirect our pursuits. It is particularly important to provide significant instruction to those who are beginning to experience the ministry of the Holy Spirit. It is far too common for immature Christians to become boastful and equate their experience with maturity, with authority, or with an exclusive understanding of how the Holy Spirit works. This can lead to division and distraction.

False Teacher
False teachers are those that dispense messages that do not reflect the heart of God. False teachers advocate things that appear to have spiritual value, yet do not. False teachers teach incomplete truth, so the message is easily accepted because it is cloaked in truth.

Demonic Instruction
1 Timothy 4 warns us that in the end times people will fall away from the faith because they will buy into the messages of "deceitful spirits and doctrines of demons," coming from false teachers who lead people astray with errant focus, like forbidding marriage and denouncing certain foods. Take note that this passage is talking about the Church! It speaks of people in The Body of Christ that leave the teachings of truth and begin enforcing Pharisaical standards. We expect the world to be under the sway and influence of the wicked one, but this is a sobering picture of the way the enemy tries to infiltrate the Church, by inserting distractions that dilute or negate the message of the Gospel and cause division between God's children.

This passage, of course, also demonstrates the counter to what we read about Gabriel instructing Daniel. We need to be savvy to the fact that the enemy of our souls absolutely wants to deceive us and is actively working to do so. The doctrines of demons, according to this passage, will work their way into the Body of Christ in the end times. This reinforces the need, as the Bible clearly dictates, to test the spirits and test "truths" that surface against the Holy Scriptures to see if they hold water.

Summary

What then is the purpose of growing in your specifically designed role in the Body of Christ? Is it to pigeonhole yourself, become myopic, and refuse to participate in any ministry that doesn't fit your role? No, my friend, it is to be able to focus in on the passions that God has ignited deep in your soul and provide you a framework for employing those passions. If your passion is for helping people understand the truth of Scripture, then maybe your role is that of a teacher. Knowing this, as you begin to discover Him in the Word, the Spirit of God within you becomes more recognizable as He shows you increasing opportunities to teach others, moment by moment, throughout your day. Now, it will likely occur that some of that teaching may be with someone who is not yet part of the Body of Christ. Maybe your small teaching moment with them conveys the perfect truth that they needed to hear to lead them to Christ. You have just participated in evangelism, even though your role is inherently as a teacher.

How do you begin to identify your role in the Body of Christ? It may be helpful to ask the question, "What 'Kingdom' passion has He given me?" Are you passionate about advancing the Kingdom of God? That may indicate that you are wired as an apostle. Are you passionate about repentance and revival? Your role may be that of a prophet. Are you passionate about reaching the lost? You may be an evangelist. Are you passionate about illuminating the Word of God to His children? You may be a teacher. Are you passionate about reconciling and restoring believers to their Heavenly Father? You may be called to be a pastor.

Knowing your role is not the "end-all." It is simply meant to be a catalyst. At the end of the day, we do not want to limit or restrict God by listing how He will or won't use us. However, knowing some specific truths about how He designed us can be a very liberating factor in our engaging in the Kingdom and discovering our calling.

CHAPTER 10

AUTHENTIC VS. COUNTERFEIT: SPIRITUAL GIFTS

"I became convinced that denominational explanations of the Gifts were all tainted by their individual doctrines. I prayed for His filling, on His terms. I wanted Him to define gifting for me, and He began to."

The gifts of the Spirit are characteristics of God that are activated by God within His children, at His discretion, and in a very telling sequence: 1. Inwardly, in the life of the believer, for restoration and healing with the Father (Romans 8:26-30), 2. In the Church, for the unifying and equipping of the saints (1 Corinthians 14:24,25), and 3. In the Kingdom of God, for a sign to the world (1 Corinthians 14:22).

The very principal reason that the Body of Christ experiences the gifts of the Spirit is above all else, an "inward" reason. It is to knit our spirits to His Spirit. In this close state of engagement and vulnerability, the Father ministers to our hearts through His Spirit. Remember that part of Jesus' mission was to heal the brokenhearted. This primary work of the Spirit is where He prepares us for fellowship, He prepares us for battle, and He prepares us for Kingdom advancement. If we do not acknowledge the significance and validity of this process in the Spirit, we will not be equipped for the destiny we have been created for. Differing, yet complimentary, members of the Body function together to illuminate where God is working within His people. As Paul writes in Romans 1:11,12, "For I long to see you so that I may impart some spiritual gift to you, that you may be established; that is, that I may be encouraged together with you while among you, each of us by the other's faith, both yours and mine."

1 Corinthians 14:12 exhorts us, "So also you, since you are zealous of spiritual gifts, seek to abound for the edification of the church."

The inevitable result of the Body ministering inwardly to its members is a unity that is unrivaled by the typical superficial connections we currently experience. Jesus, in His famous prayer from John 17, emotes to the Father, "The glory which You have given Me I have given to them, that they may be one, just as We are one; I in them and You in Me, that they may be perfected in unity, so that the world may know that You sent Me, and loved them, even as You have loved Me." When we are this united in His Spirit, our inward ministry overflows and turns into an outpouring.

Such an outpouring of the Spirit through the Body of Christ is exactly what the enemy wants to keep from happening. These outpourings of the Spirit of God have changed the course of history through revivals and movements-always bringing people to reconciliation with the Father. Many of the gifts are quiet and understated, while a few are quite visible and are designed for dramatic effect, to advance the Kingdom of God.

Ultimately, the "proper" use of gifts happens when we have first experienced the restorative work of the Spirit in our own life. To paraphrase A.W. Tozer in "Whatever Happened to Worship," we have no platform to minister to others if we ourselves have not experienced God. When we minister through this filter, we are ministering through the Father's agenda, not our own. There is no room for selfish motivation in the use of the gifts. Conversely, when we wield the gifts of our own volition, we do so at extreme risk of misrepresenting the heart of God, and that my friends, is a false usage of the gifts of the Spirit. How much of our aversion to "spirit-filled" people is based on this experience? Misrepresentation of God happens all the time by well meaning Christians, but ultimately, by Christians who are not yet yielded to the Father's will.

This chapter is not so much written to be a tutorial on how to use the gifts, but rather, in keeping with the theme of this book, to illustrate the ways that the Holy Spirit operates and the ways that the Adversary tries to distort and confuse through his counterfeits.

Discernment vs. Sensuality

Discernment
"But solid food is for the mature, who because of practice have their senses trained to discern good and evil." Hebrews 5:14

Thayer defines discerning as "distinguishing," like how we assess or evaluate things. Our ability to evaluate something is based on our familiarity with the standard-it is what we compare everything against. For the believer, we must know the original if we are to effectively discern the counterfeit. The Greek word for discerning is the same word that is used for testing spirits. It implies our ability to assess the nature or the source of certain fruits, gifts, perspectives, agendas, and empowerments.

We Christians tend to view discernment as a process that is based in intuition, whereas *testing spirits* is based on our knowledge of Scripture. The Bible does not seem to draw much of a distinction between the two, but rather encourages us to distinguish all things using all our faculties, not just our intellect.

In 1 John 4:1, we are told to be students of the Word so that we can distinguish godly teachers from false teachers. However, the verse immediately preceding the "testing spirits" passage talks about abiding, and about the Spirit that God has given us. It is the Spirit of God within us that enables us to test other spirits. This is where discernment comes into the picture.

Scripture places discernment in the context of the Holy Spirit being in us, facilitating our "abiding" in the Father. What is abiding again? Abiding is the state of intimacy where we hear our Heavenly Father's voice and we respond to His invitations: invitations to join Him, to fight, to be comforted, to discern, etc. Remember, our spirit is in constant connection and communion with the Father through the omnipresence of Jesus Christ (1 John 2:1) and the indwelling presence of the Holy Spirit (Romans 8:26), both of whom are praying for us and our exact needs. I would say that our needs include the illumination of the workings of the enemy that wars against our hearts. Scripture describes over and over how people discern on multiple levels: through our intellect, through our intuition, as well as through our sight, hearing, and other senses (Mark 2:8, 1 Sam.9:9, 2 Kings 6:15-17, 1 Sam. 3:1-10, Is. 11:3, Job, 4:15,16, Ps. 119:103). So then, discernment is not only an intellectual comparison of truth against lies, it is also the employment of all our faculties to the same purpose.

We are told in Hebrews 5:14 that a mature Christian should be able to discern using his or her senses. It does not simply mean our intuition. It says *senses*, plural: sight, hearing, taste, smell, touch, and intuition (our sixth sense). This is a righteous, redeemed usage of the physical bodies we were given to steward. If my body is the temple of the Holy Spirit, then my senses may accurately be called the "greeters" at the doors, watchful of anything that wants to infiltrate this temple.

In this context, we are calling sensuality the direct counterfeit of discernment. Both of them employ the senses, but for what purpose?

Sensuality
If God has reserved these significant roles for our senses to play in the spiritual realm, then the counterfeit has to be the role the enemy calls our senses to in opposition to God. It is not a difficult task, as our flesh is quick to want to please itself, so the enemy facilitates opportunity. Indulgence is the name of the game, from lust at all levels, to greed, to gluttony; our senses know they were made for a greater experience than what the everyday life provides, and it is easiest to go the route of quick and cheap gratification.

Word of Wisdom vs. Demonic wisdom

Word of Wisdom
A word of wisdom[69] is the specific understanding of a matter as enabled by the Spirit. It often brings clarity or application to a word of knowledge.

King Solomon displayed divine wisdom in the famous example of the two mothers who argued over a baby, both claiming it to be their own. In wisdom, he ordered the baby be separated in half, and half be given to each woman. The true mother gave up her right to the baby in order to preserve its life, and Solomon knew she was the rightful mother. "When all Israel heard of the judgment which the king had handed down, they feared the king, for they saw that the wisdom of God was in him to administer justice." 1 Kings 3:16-28

Demonic Wisdom
There is a reason why God tells us not to follow wisdom from the world and from unbelievers. They do not understand the things of the Spirit, and they can only counsel from their flesh, their interpretation of truth, or from demonic influence.[70] I am reminded of a scripture that my mom had me memorize when I was young, Psalm 1:1.

"How blessed is the man who does not walk in the counsel of the wicked..."

Paul contrasts these two types of wisdom when he challenges the Corinthians to resolve their disputes between Christians and to not take their matters before the world for judgment. He poses a poignant question to them, "Do you not know that we will judge angels? How much more matters of this life?"[71]

Word of Knowledge vs. Lies

Word of Knowledge
What is a word of knowledge?[72] It is the very specific knowing of a pinpoint, targeted matter as revealed by the Spirit. It is practical information, useful for the identification of a matter.

---

[69] 1 Corinthians 12:8

[70] James 3:14,15

[71] 1 Corinthians 6:1-6

[72] 1 Corinthians 12:8

In Acts 5, God gave Peter a word of knowledge, that Ananias and Sapphira had lied about the sale of their property and were pretending to have tithed the full amount. In 2 Samuel 12, God gave Nathan a word of knowledge about King David's adultery and act of murder. God imparts specific knowledge for His purpose and for the furthering of His kingdom. In the two cases mentioned above, they happened to deal with hidden sin, but there are certainly many other ways that the Holy Spirit uses a word of knowledge. In what way have you experienced this in your life, either as the messenger or the recipient?

Lies

In 2 Corinthians 11, Paul the Apostle spends a considerable amount of time cautioning his spiritual children against subtle lies, crafted by the enemy to pull them slightly off target. Paul is concerned that the Church will be distracted from the simplicity of a childlike faith, and the purity of being wholly devoted to Jesus Christ. My friends, this is the same message we are conveying through this book. Being wholly devoted to Christ requires an emptying of self, otherwise, we are only partially devoted. Paul knew firsthand that one's own agenda must be renounced, and in return, that man would know the power and authority of Jesus Himself. Simply put, the enemy of our souls doesn't have to try very hard. All he has to do is to shift our focus a bit to performance, legalism, emotionalism, and the like, all in the name of Christianity, and presto! We are ineffective and unaware of that reality.

Faith in God vs. Faith in faith

Faith in God

Faith is an overused term and an underused gift these days. People "have" faith, "keep" the faith, "come to" faith, and so on and so forth. Faith, depending on the context, can mean several different things. Nowadays, faith is generally thought of as another term for "religion."

In the context of spiritual gifts, faith becomes much more than a synonym for "Christianity." It is also more than just *consistency* and *endurance*, as in *keeping the faith*. Finally, it is much more than the general faith that Christians are called to have in Jesus; "It is written, 'The righteous shall live by faith.'"

Faith, as a spiritual gift, is a special invitation and directive to trust God for a specific situation and outcome. The gift of faith is also a prerequisite to miraculous gifts. Remember Jesus' words after healing the centurion's servant? "Truly I say to you, I have not found such great faith with anyone in Israel."[73]

Many times, a person with the gift of faith is enabled to have faith on behalf of another person, as in the story of the paralytic whose friends tore open a hole in a roof to lower him down to Jesus.[74]

A while back, I had a dream about a friend. It was a short dream, but there was a real sense of urgency to it, as my friend in this dream was in a critical situation. I woke up and prayed for this friend, but I remained confused about the occurrence. I don't frequently get dreams from the Lord. Was this from Him? If so, what was I supposed to do with it? I had a lot of questions, and as it turned out, I was going to meet with a mentor that following day. I decided to ask her opinion of the matter, and she prefaced her response with her own similar experience.

Suzan was an executive with a major American corporation and was in Washington D.C. on business many years ago. After a long day, she remembers taking the subway back to her hotel. As she sat in her seat, she couldn't help but notice a man sitting across from her and down the aisle. He appeared to be consumed in thought, and a sense of heaviness seemed to engulf him. She watched him get off at his stop, and wondered what could be consuming him.

Later, in the middle of the night, Suzan was awakened by the Lord with a heaviness and urgency to pray. This man was paramount on her heart. She didn't understand the nature of the urgency at first, but she started to get a sense that this man was contemplating suicide. She prayed for this man for about 30 minutes, when the heaviness finally lifted. The understanding she received from the Lord was that the moment of crisis had passed for this man.

God had invited Suzan to have faith on behalf of this man. He was certainly not in a position to be rational, let alone have the slightest bit of hope. And, as we know, hope is evidence of faith. If there is no faith, there can be no hope. If there is hope, then there is, no matter how slight, faith in an outcome beyond our current understanding. This man had no hope and no faith. God invited Suzan to join this man and Himself in this process, and for her to be his champion.

Why would God need to do this? Why wouldn't He just take care of this man directly? For reasons known only to Himself, He seems to delight in

---

[73] Matthew 8:5-10

[74] Mark 2:1-5

allowing believers to partner with Him, and God frequently invites us to join Him for no other reason than to benefit us. Knowing this has certainly made me more aware of opportunities, like my dream, to join Him where He is at work.

You may have faith that God can use you to heal someone. Do you also have faith that God may not want to heal that same person? That is much harder. Yet, the reality is that this is all about *His* agenda and *His* glory. Remember, He promises to give us whatever we ask when it is aligned with *His* will. That is always the qualifier. Always.

Faith in Faith

Faith in faith itself is a subtle counterfeit, to be sure. The main evidence, and therefore, the main problem with it is that validation comes from one's faithfulness, rather than from our true hope, Jesus Christ. A person who is trapped in the snare of trusting in faith is often quite dutiful in their repetition of religious observances: attending church services multiple times per week, repetitive prayers, adherence to traditions, etc. Now, that is not to say that any of these things are wrong in and of themselves, but, they are commonly embraced by those who place stock in their own faithfulness. Jesus called the Pharisees out on the carpet for this very thing, even going so far as to say that their "worship" and practices were in vain, since they were teaching their own fabrications as though they were gospel truth.[75]

Healing vs. Demonic Healing

Divine Healing

God loves to heal people. Healing was a central part of Jesus' ministry. He empowered His disciples to heal, and healing is one of the spiritual gifts. Divine Healing is precise, and it is permanent. It can be either immediate or may take place over a timeframe that God determines. My experience is that God sometimes *relieves* pain as well. Is this the same as healing? Is it a matter of semantics? As always, all the glory and attention goes to God Himself. In some cases, healing comes as a result of the elimination of disease, while in other cases, it comes with forgiveness of sin or exorcism of a demon.

A dear friend of ours, who I'll call "Steve," recently told me about an experience he had. He knew of a young woman from church who had been diagnosed with cancer. Her family has a history of this kind of cancer, and she was scheduled for a hospital stay in order to assess the extent of the disease. At some point during the woman's stay at the

---

[75] Mark 7:3-8

hospital, Steve received a strong prompting from God to go to the hospital and pray, and to specifically "push back the darkness." Steve obeyed, and on entering the hospital had a strong understanding of the darkness that permeated that building. Steve, the whole way to the room, prayed and stood in authority against the enemy, clearing the heaviness and oppression as he went. Upon arriving at the woman's room, Steve spent some time with her and finally prayed over her, specifically to free her for the work of the Holy Spirit, and then he left.

About a week or so passed, and Steve happened to talk with the secretary from the church. She perked up and asked him, "Steve, did you hear about so-and-so? She is cancer-free!" Steve was stunned. He hadn't gone there specifically to heal her. He had simply listened and obeyed. He had unwittingly been used by the Lord to heal this woman. She is cancer-free to this day.

Demonic Healing
Demonic healing is supernatural, and may even resemble divine healing. It may occur through a "faith healer" in its subtle form, or through shamans or psychic surgeons at the more extreme end of the spectrum. An interesting concept to consider is the possibility that the enemy can and does cause physical harm and illness. Remember the story from Matthew 17? "When they came to the crowd, a man came up to Jesus, falling on his knees before Him and saying, "Lord, have mercy on my son, for he is a lunatic and is very ill; for he often falls into the fire and often into the water...And Jesus rebuked him, and the demon came out of him, and the boy was cured at once." Consider this; the enemy can cause illness and, at the opportune moment, remove the illness for his own deceptive purposes. Why would he do this? Mark 13:22 explains, "For false christs and false prophets will arise, and will show signs and wonders, in order to lead astray, if possible, the elect." Again, this reinforces the reality that the enemy wants to distract and mislead the Church. He knows that his approach must be subtle to have the desired effect.

The Bible refers to a few situations where sick people were condemned by God because they did not go to Him for healing, but to the counterfeit: Ahaziah[76] and Asa[77] are two examples from the Bible.

Miracles vs. Magic

When it comes to the subject of miracles, we instantly think of the

---

[76] 2 Kings 1:2

[77] 2 Chronicles 16:12

miracles that Jesus performed. We create some distance in our minds regarding these miracles, as Jesus was perfect. We tend to think, "Of course He could perform them." Let's put aside what we know about Jesus' authority and how He modeled it to us, and how the Father has promised us the same authority. For the purposes of this chapter, let us focus instead on miracles performed by regular folks in the Bible.

Do you remember the story of Moses? He was a regular guy. "No he wasn't," you may think. "Moses was raised in a palace, ruled as a prince, saw God, and he even wrote part of the Bible." Well, sure, this is all true, but we are essentially jumping from A to Z. Do you remember the part where he killed someone, ran from the law, and lived as a fugitive in the desert? Do you remember the point where God appeared to Moses, completely uninitiated by anything that Moses had done? Moses was hiding, remember? Moses protested at God's plans, reminding God that he had a speech impediment or dyslexia, or some other physical trait that made him embarrassed to be heard.

How about the fact that up until this point in recorded history, humans had not performed miracles? Sure, we see the amazing activity of God before this, but He invites Moses, regular, timid, escapist Moses, to be empowered to do an impossible task. God enables Moses to perform miracles and directs Moses throughout the process of emancipating the Israelites from Egyptian rule. Let's take a look at just one of the miracles that God initiated, as well as the counterfeit that the Egyptian magicians reacted with.

Miracle
God told Moses that Pharaoh would challenge him to perform a supernatural act. When he did so, Moses was to instruct Aaron to throw down his walking stick in front of Pharaoh and that is would transform into a snake. When the time came, Pharaoh did provoke, and Moses and Aaron responded as God had instructed.[78]

Magic
Of course, this was the great showdown and Pharaoh couldn't let this go. Pharaoh was worshipped as a god himself. He couldn't let an outlaw shepherd from an inferior people and culture show him up! Since Pharaoh wasn't able to mimic this supernatural act personally, he demanded his sorcerers, wise men and magicians to conjure up a counterfeit. When their occultic power finally produced the counterfeit

---

[78] Exodus 7:8-10

they were attempting, God made Aaron's rod swallow up all of theirs.[79] Miracles occur at God's decree and for His purpose, and He has always included His people in His work.

Prophecy vs. Divination

Prophecy is a much stigmatized gift. When we think of prophecy, we typically default to an image of someone in the Old Testament issuing random, yet profound statements on behalf of the Lord. We most often equate prophecy with the foretelling of future events, and we tend to relegate prophecy almost exclusively to the Old Testament. This description of prophecy is accurate, but is incomplete.

This is the most accurate description of prophecy that I have come across. I believe it does a great job of dispelling the myth that prophecy is all about foretelling the future:

> "By simply picking verses from the prophets and pasting them together to give "prophecies that prove the Bible" or "Jesus Christ in prophecy," one creates the impression that prophecy is "history written in advance." However, when one studies the prophets, this glamorous concept suddenly disappears. It is necessary to plow through chapters that have nothing to do with the future in order to find a single verse, or even part of a verse, that is "prophecy."

> "...God is never concerned with the present simply for the sake of that moment. Ever since creation, he has been working out his purpose for humankind, and he never forgets where he is going and what he is doing. The prophets are let in on that purpose (Amos 3:7). Prophecy is therefore not simply God's message to the present situation, but is intended primarily to show how that situation fits into his plan, how he will use it to judge and refine or comfort and encourage his people. Prophecy is God's message to the present in the light of his ongoing redemptive purpose.

> On exceptional occasions, he gives rather precise details about what he is going to do. Yet even in this instruction, usually called "predictive prophecy," the predictive element is almost always firmly attached to the present situation. The prophet speaks about what has meaning for his listeners. He does not suddenly forget them and utter an irrelevant "prophecy of things to come." Rather, he takes them from that moment into the sweep of divine

---

[79] Exodus 7:11,12

redemptive activity and centers on a truth that will become a beacon to God's people."[80]

As 2 Peter 1:21 states, "No prophecy was ever made by an act of human will, but men moved by the Holy Spirit spoke from God." Prophecy is simply the Holy Spirit facilitating God's speaking through men and women. "How is this different than a word of Knowledge?" you may ask. Susan Jerome of Pastoral Care Ministries explains it this way. "Knowledge is concrete, pin-pointed, practical and identifying. Prophecy uncovers, it reveals intent, it announces, and it allows the Lord to speak into a matter. In a simple metaphor, if Knowledge opens the door, then Prophecy turns on the light."

Prophecy

Jesus Himself promised that, just as Peter describes above, the Holy Spirit will speak through us at His appointed times.[81] Prophecy, like a word of knowledge or a word of wisdom, is simply "speaking as the Lord speaks."[82] God uses regular people to prophecy. They don't even have to be a "prophet." As Amos profoundly states, "I am not a prophet, nor am I the son of a prophet; for I am a herdsman and a grower of sycamore figs. But the LORD took me from following the flock and the LORD said to me, 'Go prophesy to My people Israel'" Amos 7:14,15.

The gifts of the Spirit serve to bring and bond people to the Father. Prophecy does so by illuminating the condition of our hearts through the brightness of God's holiness. 1 Corinthians 14:24,25 capture this truth succinctly, "But if all prophesy, and an unbeliever or an ungifted man enters, he is convicted by all, he is called to account by all; *the secrets of his heart are disclosed*; and so he will fall on his face and worship God, declaring that God is certainly among you."

Some time ago, God woke Desiree up in the night and gave her a scripture reference. It happened to be one that meant something to her in the past, but that night she didn't understand the purpose of the verse. The following day the Lord prompted her to skip her prayer group and to instead go to the local coffee shop. As she sat there, God directed her to share that scripture with a young couple at a nearby table. Des gave the woman the scripture and a message about what God was about to bring

---

[80] "Old Testament Survey" by William Sanford La Sor, David Allan Hubbard, Frederic William Bush pp. 304, 305

[81] Matthew 10:18-20

[82] Numbers 24:13

about in her life. This couple was astounded at the clarity and directness of the message. They went on to tell Desiree that they too had been prompted that evening to get out of the house, and that they had driven miles and miles to a few different locations before God directed them to that specific coffee shop. This is one example of prophecy.

Another example involves a friend of mine that I'll call "David." David approached me one Sunday after church and he told me that he had a dream about me the previous night. It was dark and heavy. There were ominous storm clouds over my shoulder in the evening sky. When he awoke, he asked the Lord what the dream was about, and the Lord placed an urgency on his heart to communicate a message to me, "Brandon, do not fear." David shared these words with me, and since I have developed a trust with David, I valued his words. I just didn't know what they meant. It would be six months before God reminded me that He sent David specifically to give me that message ahead of time, as I experienced the darkest, heaviest, most anxious time of my life.

False Prophecy
Counterfeit prophecy in the Bible takes a few different forms: Divination, where a demon is feeding a person information about current or future events,[83] False Prophecy, where prophets fabricate claims of divine revelation,[84] and Deception, where God Himself allows misguiding words to flow from the mouths of false prophets as a consequence of disobedience.[85]

Tongues: Spirit-led vs. Self-led

Tongues are a divisive topic, to say the least. Tongues have become even more of a point of division in the modern church than they were in the early church. Some claim that tongues are evidence of salvation, others claim that tongues are simply one of the spiritual gifts the Holy Spirit uses, and still others claim that they do not exist at all. We will take a brief look at a topic that has been sharply debated far longer than we have been around. We are not looking to support any particular denominational view, rather, we are simply looking to validate the evidence the Scriptures present.

---

[83] Acts 16:16-18

[84] Ezekiel 13:1-3, 6-8

[85] 1 Kings 22:1-24

Spirit-led

We are told in 1 Corinthians 12:28 that there are various kinds of tongues. I believe the Scriptures clearly represent two different kinds of tongues: foreign language and prayer language.

Regarding the first kind, tongues as a foreign language, we conservatives tend to acknowledge this type as legitimate, while we have a hard time accepting the other type. Foreign language tongues were used by the Holy Spirit early in the Book of Acts, as the Apostles were enabled to communicate with foreigners in their own languages.[86] The Greek root of this form of tongues is *xenoglossy*, which means "foreign tongue."

Referencing the second kind, prayer language, Paul gives us his perspective. This kind, he says, is not to speak to men, but to God.[87] Paul minimizes the significance of this kind of tongues because no one understands them, yet, he immediately reinforces how he wishes that they all spoke in these tongues. These tongues, he states, are how his spirit prays.[88] But, as he goes on to state, these tongues are unfruitful both to his mind and to the hearer. He challenges the Christians who spoke in these tongues to also worship with their minds and to pray also for the ability to interpret, so that they may edify the rest of the body. The Greek root of this form of tongues is *glossolalia*, which refers to the verbalizing of unintelligible sounds in a state of religious excitement.[89]

My dad was mentored over the course of two decades by an inspirational man of God, Leonard Ravenhill. Leonard was an old school English revivalist preacher. My father recounted to me what Leonard had to say about his own experience with tongues. He said that he had, in his own special times alone with God, spoken in tongues on a variety of occasions, after simply running out of words to express his adoration of the Father. In his case, it was always private, and always special.

Paul's concern over the practice of prayer language tongues seems to be the same as ours today. He is concerned over the usage of this prayer language: no one else understands it (unlike the foreign language tongues), in and of itself it does not encourage or edify, and worse yet, it

---

[86] Acts 2:4-6

[87] 1 Corinthians 14:2

[88] 1 Corinthians 14:14

[89] Columbia Encyclopedia

can be perceived as crazy.[90] According to Susan Jerome of Pastoral Care Ministries, the way she has publicly seen tongues best edify the Church is when there is already a very strong presence and activity of the Lord, and a mature Christian delivers a message from the Lord in tongues, it is interpreted, and it ushers people forward into communion with God. In these cases, tongues bring a message in the Spirit, generally an invitation and prompting from God for the congregation to fall in with Him.

I once had an amazing experience with a fellow brother in Christ. We had been meeting for a while, examining his perspectives and misconceptions about what God thinks of him. We normally engaged in great discussion, like iron sharpening iron, but that day was different. I sensed a prompting by the Holy Spirit that the Heavenly Father was wanting to speak truth to "Phil," so we asked God where He wanted to start. He reminded us of the lie that was principle in Phil's life, robbing him of connecting with his Father in Heaven. As we prayed together, it was clear that the enemy was not going to relinquish this stronghold without a fight. I was prompted to stand up and symbolically take a stand against the enemy. As I stood with arms outstretched, "pushing back the opposition," I prayed for the Father to reveal His truth to "Phil." He then prompted me to ask for the Holy Spirit to fall and pour into us. As soon as the words were prayed, I felt something pouring over me, onto my head, down through my center, and then out toward Phil. It was a powerful, deliberate, and focused flow of the Holy Spirit through me. I have experienced this before, but in much more limited ways; it felt like very strong tingling, but with movement. It was stronger than the tingling that you experience when your hand falls asleep: annoying, stationary and superficial. This was enrapturing, it was moving in me, and it ran deep within me. I was instantly overcome, and the tears began flowing down my cheeks. The Spirit was clearly flowing through me and into Phil. I could hear something happening with him, but I did not want to look and risk quenching the Spirit. Phil, a life-long conservative Christian, began speaking in tongues in that moment. It was quiet, it was private, and it was a special moment between him and his Father. As Phil found his place with his Heavenly Father, his Abba, his Daddy, the Spirit brought a deep stillness and peace to our communion. All was quiet as Phil sat with his Daddy and received perfect love from Him. Needless to say, God used a powerful encounter in the Holy Spirit to drive home the intellectual truth that Phil received that day. Why would He do this? I believe He did so because the lie was so strong, and Phil would need proof of the truth. As my dad reminded me the other day, "A man with an experience is

---

[90] 1 Corinthians 14:23

never at the mercy of a man with an argument." Phil experienced God. It was real, and no one or nothing can take it from him. Praise be to God, the Author and Perfecter of our faith!

Self-led
I believe the reason for such debate over tongues is based in the ignoring of Paul's instructions. When people dismiss the guidelines found in 1 Corinthians 14 and choose to speak in tongues without an interpreter, or when they speak in tongues in a disruptive manner, it reflects a selfish spirit. The motives of man are in play, and we know that this is a sure way to quench the work of the Holy Spirit. The result is often mayhem, confusion, and as Paul warned of, a lack of edification or encouragement.

I remember visiting a charismatic church many years ago with a friend. Long after the praise songs had started, he continued chatting with another friend about some trivial matter. As soon as he had finished talking to his friend, he started speaking in tongues, joining others in the commotion of this church service. I was certainly confused. If tongues is a "prayer language," I wondered, and it is in place to express the depths of our connection with the Father, then how in the world can a person jump from a trite conversation into such a meaningful communion in the Spirit? Needless to say, there was no interpretation, and the moment only served to frustrate me. Was the application of this gift done in error and immaturity, or was it not actually gifting in the first place? Moments of intimacy, as well as moments of true spiritual empowerment, depend on us joining our Father. This means we must submit our motives and perspectives to His, so that we may proceed on His terms, for His purpose, and with the empowerment of the Holy Spirit.

Interpretations: Spirit-led vs. Self-led

Divine Interpretation
Interpretation is the unveiling and demystifying of dreams and tongues. The reality is that the implementation of these gifts occurs everyday, on a much more mundane level. Consider this; if you are intent on abiding in the Spirit and listening for His prompting, He will certainly enable these areas of giftedness as He sees fit. Joseph,[91] Daniel,[92] and Gideon's friend[93] interpreted in the Old Testament, and we are assured that the

---

[91] Genesis 41:11

[92] Daniel 5

[93] Judges 7:13

same would continue to happen in the New Testament.[94] Interpretations can apply to both dreams and to prayer language tongues, as well as any other application the Spirit chooses to illuminate.

Demonic Interpretation
In Deuteronomy 18:10, the children of Israel were warned about several pagan practices, one of which was that of interpreting omens. This would be similar to today's tarot card readers, tea-leaf readers, crystal ball seers, Ouija board users, etc.[95] A Christian is to have no part of such demonic influence.

Exhortation: Spirit-led vs. Self-led

Spirit-led
Exhortation is the act of encouraging, propelling, and even helping a person "get back on the path." When it is performed at the prompting of the Holy Spirit, it has pin-pointed accuracy. Paul describes having to set Peter straight and get him back into alignment with God in Galatians 2, when Peter started behaving in a two-faced manner toward the Gentiles in front of his Jewish colleagues. Spirit-led exhortation is highly constructive, even when having to deliver a corrective message.

Self-led
Unfortunately, it is quite easy to react to people and situations out of our own perspective. It is too easy to respond to people in a manner that we think is righteous, all the while doing a disservice to the Holy Spirit's agenda. We see a couple of examples of this in the New Testament with Jesus' disciples. In one case they rebuked little children from distracting Jesus,[96] and in another case, they prevented people from casting demons out because they were not part of the disciples' "in-crowd."[97] Jesus had to set them straight in both cases. In both cases, it was their own perspectives that were dictating how they "exhorted" people.

Giving: Spirit-led vs. Self-led

Spirit-led
Have you ever been prompted by the Holy Spirit to give something away? I have certainly experienced this. He seems to be pretty specific

---

[94] 1 Corinthians 12:10

[95] "Commentary on Deuteronomy 18," by David Guzik

[96] Mark 10:13

[97] Mark 9:38

when He prompts me in this capacity. If He is prompting me to give money to someone, He tells me how much. In fact, that is a sort of barometer for me as to whether I am being prompted by the Spirit or whether my mind is leading me. If the prompting is to give the homeless man at the coffee shop $20, I have learned to give it more credence than just a generic thought that "you should help this guy." Spirit-led giving is energizing, even if it costs us dearly. Paul reminds us of this as he praises the Macedonian churches in 2 Corinthians 8 for their liberal giving in the face of their circumstances.

Self-led
Self-led giving is a good thing, but not a God thing. Our own selfish motives can look noble at times. Ananias and Sapphira both gave on selfish terms. Sometimes we give for the accolade. Sometimes we give because it is easier than serving. Sometimes we give because we want a particular outcome. I have been guilty of this myself. We have to inquire of the Lord to be sure we are giving according to His will.

Leading: Spirit-led vs. Self-led

Spirit-led
Since we have gifts that differ according to the grace given to us, each of us is to exercise them accordingly: if prophecy, according to the proportion of his faith; if service, in his serving; or he who teaches, in his teaching; or he who exhorts, in his exhortation; he who gives, with liberality; he who leads, with diligence; he who shows mercy, with cheerfulness. Romans 12:6-8

What is God-designed leadership? Leadership is the ability to initiate, originate, launch, create, inspire and organize. It is different than management, as someone strong in managing can perpetuate, operate, fulfill vision, and preserve a movement.

Leadership is a profound responsibility. There are so many people that want to be seen as leaders, and exert a lot of energy to be perceived that way. And, there are others that truly do not want it, yet it consistently seems like people want to fall in line behind them. I think that just as "the last will be first and the first, last," that God enjoys raising up the underdog to a place of great expectation, great stretching, great burden, and yet, great respect. Sometimes, but not always, great leadership requires a person not born with great confidence, but one who has endured the darkest of times and has emerged as an overcomer.

Self-led

A major misconception is that leadership is a personality trait. Men and women constantly buy into this lie, and as a result, they acquiesce to the singular personality type that screams "leadership:" the dominant, or "Type A" personality. This is the "alpha-male" stereotype that assumes the lead most of the time, and is often results-oriented to a fault. In general, we assume that this is a "born-leader." The reality is that these people are typically just assertive enough to be given the lead role in life. As a result, their personalities drive their activity, not necessarily their submission to the Holy Spirit.

How many of us defer leadership to people that are naturally assertive? How many of us live with the lie that we couldn't possibly be a leader? This is most definitely not from God. He has designed each of us so uniquely that only I could possibly fit the role He has created for me, and you for yours. "For we are His workmanship, created in Christ Jesus for good works, which God prepared beforehand so that we would walk in them" Ephesians 2:10. The reality is that God crafts leaders from all different types of personalities, strengths, experiences, resources and backgrounds.

Let me assure you, brothers and sisters, that choosing to remain unaware or indifferent to God's destiny for you does not excuse you from it. It is our desire, that through this book, you may better understand the activity and potential of the Holy Spirit in your life, enabling you to live out the good works that you have been prepared for, and that have been prepared for you, and to do so with the leadership perspective that comes with the authority God gives us for our calling.

As to our assertive friends, God made you perfectly for the role He reserved for you. The challenge, as it is for all of us, is to empty ourselves of our facades and agendas so we can receive all that we need from Him and be empowered to live out the destiny we are called to.

Mercy: Spirit-led vs. Self-led

Spirit-led

"When Jesus therefore saw her weeping, and the Jews who came with her also weeping, He was deeply moved in spirit and was troubled, and said, 'Where have you laid him?' They said to Him, 'Lord, come and see.' Jesus wept." John 11:33-35.

A person experiencing the gift of mercy understands what the Bible describes about Jesus in this last passage. Jesus wasn't sad about the death of Lazarus; He was about to raise him from the dead. Instead, Jesus aches for his friends, Mary and Martha. His heart breaks for them, as He takes on their pain and suffering. This is what inspires Him to weep; not the perceived "hopelessness" of the situation. Mercy isn't sympathy, it is empathy.

If you experience this gifting, you understand the significance of being empathetic. Empaths generally have to grow in understanding in this gift, learning how the Spirit intends to use it. Otherwise, they can take on an inordinate amount of pain and suffering on someone's behalf and wilt under the weight of it. In fact, I believe that "bearing one another's burdens"[98] is often intended solely for the purpose of us being able to better understand and minister to people in need.

Self-led
The enemy certainly knows how to mimic the authentic and exploit people with this sensitivity. It is all too common for a person to "take on" the burden of another person, just for the sake of easing their pain. There are some inherent problems with this. The first area of danger is when that person puts him or herself in God's role; some call this the zone of "responsibility lines." When I put myself on the line between a person and the solution, the Father, I am blocking their connection. I am to come *alongside* the person in need, not become the solution or a crutch to them.

Second, there is a hazard in taking on someone else's pain when we are not healed ourselves. Unless I am abiding and in agreement with the Spirit, I may not be able to distinguish between the person's pain and my own heart's condition. It is easy to become trapped by someone else's burden. This is an area where discernment is greatly needed.

Finally, mercy, like any other gift, is Spirit initiated. If this is truly a gift, then it has a power source. The Spirit prompts us and indicates when it is time for mercy. Just as a person with the gift of prophecy does not walk around prophesying all day long, so a person with the gift of mercy does not have mercy all day long. It is deliberate, intentional, and guided by the Spirit for whom He wants to minister. Outside of this, mercy is a good thing, but it may not be a God thing.

---

[98] Galatians 6:2

Service: Spirit-led vs. Self-led

The gift of service seems so benign, but it is probably one of the most abused gifts. When we think of gift-abuse, we often think of tongues or some other gift that is flaunted inappropriately. The gift of service, however, gets abused in some very different ways. What typically happens in a church, any church? People with this gift are singled out and taken advantage of. And, quite honestly, they allow themselves to be taken advantage of. People with this gift are often unassuming, and they sincerely just want to help. This is the first way this gift is abused. The second way is that this gift is where a lot of people hide. We'll talk more about this in the next few paragraphs.

Spirit-led
There was once a woman named Tabitha in the New Testament. She was amazing. She abundantly blessed people with a constant care for their needs. She made clothes for people. Everything she did was done with kindness and charity.[99]

As with any spiritual gift, we are impassioned and empowered by the growth and use of our gift. Those around us can attest to that gift in our life, as it is genuine and is part of who we are. That is not to say that it is always fun or exhilarating, but, when we minister in our area of gifting, we know that we are an integral part of the Body of Christ.

Self-led
There was once a different woman named Martha. We all know the story of Martha. She was a doer. And, when Jesus came to stay with her and her sister Mary, Martha was distracted with all the preparations. She was annoyed that Mary was sitting with Jesus instead of helping in the kitchen. She tried to get Jesus to see things from her perspective, but to no avail. Jesus told her, "Martha, Martha, you are worried and bothered about so many things; but only one thing is necessary, for Mary has chosen the good part, which shall not be taken away from her" Luke 10:38-42.

How many of us operate like Martha in this passage? How many of us are "busy" for Jesus? How many of us are caught in this subconscious process of "impressing" God? I believe that the gift of service is probably the most abused gift because it can happen in any denomination of church, all in the name of being a "good Christian." For many of us, however, there is a greater form of abuse.

---

[99] Acts 9:36-39

You see, we denounce "works" and those who are caught in the cycle of having to "do" things for their salvation. We would lump into that category things like counting beads, having to go to confession, mandatory missions, repetitive prayer, celibacy, pilgrimages, mortification of the flesh and self-flagellation. We know in our minds that there is no way to "earn" salvation, yet we become very dutiful and regimented in other ways to make sure we're on God's "good side." A "good" Christian has a particular image to uphold, so we engross ourselves, for as long as we think it is working, in performing for God. Service is an easy way to do it, because there are actual things that need to get done at the church facility. We can volunteer for things and earn points on some imaginary list. We believe that "great is our reward in heaven," yet we fail to put that in context. The context is always in our submission and obedience to God's invitation and gifting; remember the parable of the talents? God is not interested in us being busy; He instead wants us to "be about our Father's business."

Administration: Spirit-led vs. Self-led

Spirit-led
Administration is a gift through which either immediate or long-term needs, direction, and vision are identified for departments or ministries or a church as a whole, and the Body of Christ can be directed with clear focus.

In the Book of Acts we see an example where administration was used to solve a particular need in the church. There were widows that were missing out of the daily food ministry and needed to be provided for. The twelve apostles called a meeting and came up with a Spirit-inspired solution to the problem.[100] Some with this gift are long-term strategists. Others receive a very clear understanding of how God is wanting to move in a particular moment, and they can help "keep things on track" in partnership with the moving of the Holy Spirit.

Self-led
There are those who are gifted in this area, and there are countless more who have to operate in this capacity based on their job-description. So, in this case, I describe the "self-led" gift of administration as an occurrence that happens because someone "has" to. The dubious distinction goes to church pastors, elders and staff, because the Church is often run as a business, and people do what they are hired to do or

---

[100] Acts 6:1-7

what their job description includes. And, as with any gift, it is usually painfully clear when someone is operating in an area *outside* of their giftedness.

Closing Thoughts

The Church, the Bride of Christ, often settles for something less than the original and the authentic. We too often accept the counterfeit, assuming, perhaps hoping, that it is the real thing. Church leadership nowadays convenes to discuss bylaws and fundraisers, while authentic prayer and spiritual authority sit dusty on the shelf. This is not to say that the Church is being deliberately misled. There are many well-meaning people, just like Peter, withstanding Jesus' mission of the cross, that simply do not know that they have not yet experienced the authentic work of the Holy Spirit. They go through the motions, doing all the "right things," yet with no fruit. You and I are not exempt from this.

Church leadership and staff are no more spiritual than you and I. They have no greater access to the Holy Spirit than you and I. We are all the Body of Christ, and we all have a role to play in the Kingdom. We all are like sheep, gone astray, and our going astray often includes settling for the cheap knockoffs instead of His real thing. We cannot expect to have fruit without the filling of the Holy Spirit.

As a final note on spiritual gifts, the gifts we have discussed are a basic inventory from very clear scriptures on the topic. I know that there are other gifts that people include, such as voluntary poverty, strength, celibacy and missions. I do not doubt the validity of additional gifts, but as the purpose here is simply to compare and contrast authentic and false uses of spiritual gifts, we are just looking briefly at the core gifts the Scriptures list together.

A significant reason for this is that before our audience can imagine any additional working of the Lord, they must become acquainted with the specific and clear ways He works through concrete Scriptural reference. Only after a fellow Christian experiences the biblically founded function of the Holy Spirit will he be able to be open enough the nature of God to anticipate a unique and creative work beyond imagination.

Chapter 11

Authentic vs. Counterfeit: Supernatural Phenomena

"I do not compare myself to the enemy and take a prideful position. I simply view the enemy in relation to the Father, and they all wilt in comparison. Their trickery, while intimidating on its own, becomes absurd in the light of the Father."

In this chapter we will look at more phenomena from the Bible and examine their demonic counterfeits. Some of these concepts are polarizing, to be sure. Some of these topics are not popular to talk about. Some of these ideas intimidate people. I believe, however, that we are to be "wise as serpents" as we test all things against what the Scriptures truly say.

To some, the examples from this chapter may give the impression that we are droning on, belaboring a point that isn't very important. After all, it could be the case that none of the following examples will ever affect your life. Please allow me to explain why we are pursuing these comparisons so thoroughly.

How many of us have wilted in the face of opposition? How many of us have shied away from spiritual battle? How many of us have not obeyed the prompting of the Spirit of God, strictly out of fear? How many of us have been intimidated by the power or deviousness of the enemy? I would dare say we all have, and we have all been robbed. We have been robbed of victory! We have been robbed of opportunities to experience the activity of God, firsthand. As long as we allow fear to dominate us, we will never experience true spiritual fulfillment. We want the Body of Christ to regain its spine, its spiritual backbone, and we believe that it is critical for Christians to understand that the enemy has no power and no creativity outside of what it has seen God already do: *our* God!

Any show of power from the enemy is only a dark and distant distortion of what the Spirit of God has already done. That is why we will look at the following comparisons. We encourage you to examine the evidence, and swiftly kick to the curb any fears and hangups you may have regarding the power of the enemy. You have spiritual authority in Jesus Christ, and it is high time to claim it. It is only after we acknowledge it and believe it that we can begin to grow in it. Please bear this in mind as we examine some of the more extreme examples of the authentic and counterfeit.

Filling for a specific purpose: Spirit filling vs. Possession

The Scriptures speak several times about people being filled by a supernatural entity; for the Christian, it is the Holy Spirit who fills us, while certain others are filled by demonic spirits.

Christians receive the Holy Spirit at the point of salvation, when He begins a transformative work within us from the old creation to the new. Subsequently, as we learn to yield ourselves to God, the Holy Spirit fills us as He sees fit and for whatever purpose God chooses to be glorified in. Unfortunately, denominations have crafted differing theologies out of this Biblical concept, and as a result, Christians are forced to "choose" how the Holy Spirit will manifest Himself in their life. As a result, we sometimes feel awkward about what we are supposed to believe regarding the "Baptism with the Holy Spirit" and being "Filled with the Spirit," two Biblical descriptions of how the Holy Spirit fills us.

A separate element we should consider is the classic description of a person who is "possessed" by a demon, or "severely demonized" as others would call it. Many, if not the vast majority of Christians, bristle at the thought of a demon-possessed person and the supernatural power that often is manifested. We want you to consider the thought, "What is so incredible about that?" Why be amazed (or intimidated) by a display of demonic power? In light of the Holy Spirit filling a Christian with authority and empowering them, the demonic display truly fades in comparison to the power and majesty of God in action through His children. It is time to stop being intimidated by the counterfeit, and start walking in the authentic! Let us look first at what Scripture says about Baptism with the Holy Spirit.

Baptism and Filling with the Holy Spirit
While the Scriptures do speak of Baptism with the Spirit, people interpret the meaning differently. Some call it a "second filling." Others deny it exists, often as a rebuttal to charismatic doctrine. Scripturally speaking, however, the description the Bible gives us illustrates what the purpose and characteristics of it truly are.

Scripture tells us that John the Baptist indicated Jesus would baptize with the Holy Spirit.[101] Next, we see that Jesus prepared His disciples that they would be baptized with the Holy Spirit after His ascension.[102]

---

[101] Mark 1:6-8

[102] Acts 1:3-5

Furthermore, Baptism with the Holy Spirit was later confirmed as having been experienced by the Gentiles, not just the apostles at Pentecost.[103] Finally, we are told that Baptism with the Holy Spirit is the primary unifying element within the Church, and is the very thing that ushers us into the Body of Christ.[104]

We have to ask the obvious question, "What is all the argument about? If Scripture clearly speaks of the subject, then why does this question elicit such divisive responses?" Let's look at the two most heated positions in the simplest terms possible. Group A asserts that, based on the events of Acts 2 and Acts 10, when you are Baptized with the Holy Spirit, you begin to speak in tongues. Therefore, if you do not speak in tongues, you have not been Baptized with the Holy Spirit. Speaking in tongues, then, becomes culturally expected with Group A, and those Christians teach each other how to speak in tongues so everyone can be in community. The other side, Group B, whether they want to admit it or not, is deeply offended at the insinuation that they must not have the Holy Spirit like Group A does. Group B is also offended at what they describe as "theatrics" and "mayhem" occurring in Group A's church services. So, Group B sets out to discredit Group A and the battle lines are set.

Is it safe to say, then, that the modern description of the Baptism with the Holy Spirit is definitely NOT accomplishing the exact thing it is supposed to? Could it be that, collectively, we really don't understand it?

We propose to you a simple thought. Belief in Jesus Christ as our Savior (and repentance from our sins) *initiates* our Baptism with the Holy Spirit and in it we are sealed with the Spirit as a pledge!

The Baptism with the Holy Spirit is an amazing occurrence in that it initiates us, saved from damnation, into fellowship in the Body of Christ. But, to "coin" this term and create a doctrine around it does not seem to fit the few scriptures that do speak of it. It is not prudent to dictate how the Holy Spirit will manifest Himself each time. Nor is it wise to add criteria and description to the process beyond what the Bible portrays.

We now must ask the question, "Why do some people experience amazing manifestations of God the moment they receive the Holy Spirit? I believe the answer rests in 1 Corinthians 12:11-13, which reads, "But one and *the same Spirit works all these things, distributing to each one*

---

[103] Acts 11:15-18

[104] 1 Corinthians 12:11-13

individually just as He wills...For by one Spirit we were all baptized into one body...we were all made to drink of one Spirit." The context for experiencing amazing manifestations of God's power at the moment of salvation, the point at which we are each Baptized with the Holy Spirit, is that He manifests however He sees fit!

Now that we have looked at the Biblical portrait of this phenomenon, let us look at what the Bible has to say about being *filled with the Spirit*.

There are many passages that speak of walking, living, and remaining "filled with the Spirit." If the New Testament speaks so often on the topic, they why is it such a murky subject? If we choose to explain these passages through a classic denominational filter, then we will continually bump up against completely opposite interpretations to the scriptures.

The reality is that the Scriptures indicate *various levels of activity* of the Holy Spirit within us! We would like to propose to you three general phases of the Holy Spirit's activity within us: Indwelling, Directing and Empowering. These phases tend to correspond to our *decreasing* level of self-sufficiency, from Believing, to Abiding, then Yielding.

The Spirit of God indwells us at the point of salvation, and begins *teaching* us the fundamentals of our faith.[105] When we are living in an "abiding" state, that state of hearing His voice and learning to be led by Him, we are *directed* by the Holy Spirit.[106] When we are living in a "yielded" state, we are *empowered* by the Holy Spirit with an authority that *only* comes with yieldedness.[107]

Regardless of what we choose to call it, the Spirit of God engages with us differently at different stages in our spiritual journey.

To be described as "Spirit-filled" nowadays means that you probably belong to a charismatic or Pentecostal denomination. It has become a polarized term that ignites debate over whether the characteristics of the early church are applicable at all today.

Yet, if we behave as students of the word, which we Evangelicals tend to pride ourselves on being, we have to look at the whole of Scripture. The Spirit of God is mighty and active throughout the Old Testament and the

---

[105] Ephesians 1:13

[106] 1 John 2:27, Matthew 10:19,20

[107] John 3:30, John 14:12-15

New. And the theology of being filled with the Spirit is not one that is limited in Scripture to the early church in the Book of Acts. Rather, it is a theme that plays consistently throughout the whole Bible.

Demonic Possession

Of course, we see the enemy "filling" people for his purpose as well, and demon possession, or demonization as some prefer to call it, is generally what we think of in this context. There are plenty of examples throughout Scripture documenting this reality. And, in keeping with one of the emphases of this book, we must concede that we have given an unbalanced weight to demonization *over* the power of the Holy Spirit in the life of a child of God.

Why is this? If we look factually at the matter, demonization is the counterfeit. The original is the filling of God Himself into a human being. The activity of the Holy Spirit within us is infinitely more powerful than the influence of a demon in an unbeliever. Do we not remember the words of 1 John 4:4, "You are from God, little children, and have overcome them; because greater is He who is in you than he who is in the world?"

In John 13:27, we see Satan entering Judas. This was a pivotal moment in history, and Satan certainly wouldn't give another demon the pleasure of causing Jesus harm. However, in our experience, it will more likely be demon possession or demonization that keeps an unbelieving person under the influence of the wicked one.

When we think of demon-possession, how many of us instantly think of Legion, the man with many demons from Mark 5:1-19. We think of craziness and danger, perhaps even a person who is completely uncontrollable. While this does happen, I believe that spirit-filling by the enemy is much more common than people consider. After all, concerning clairvoyants, mediums, psychics, witches and others like them, who is empowering them? They likely appear quite normal and functional, but they have been filled, enabled, empowered, etc, by the wicked one.

The point of all this is to assert that Christians, filled with the Spirit, have authority far beyond any of these people. We have the authentic! They only have the cheap imitation. We are filled by *the* Deity of the Universe! They are only filled by a created spirit. There is no comparison! "Greater is He who is in us, than he who is in the world!"

Spirit translocation vs. Astral projection

We again look at an otherworldly topic, this time, the topic of spirit travel: the ability of a person's spirit to depart the body by choice or by enabling and return once again to re-inhabit. There exists a debate over whether or not actual travel occurs by a person's spirit, or whether it is a fabrication by a supernatural entity. In the case of the Holy Spirit, instances of spirit translocation, or the transport of a human spirit into an otherwise inaccessible supernatural location, like Heaven, appear very similar in nature to a vision. Hence arises the question, did John on the island of Patmos *actually* travel in the spirit, or was it simply a vision? On the flip-side, we ask the same questions regarding astral projection. Are practitioners *actually* enabled to travel outside the body, or is the entire experience a lie? Lies are, of course, the specialty of the enemy. Could astral projection be nothing more than a fabrication of demonic origin? Does the answer really matter? Not really. Anything demonic in nature is to be denounced. Any demonic experience is a counterfeit. So, in focusing instead on the divine, are we to pursue a potential experience of spirit travel? Of course not. As we continue to state, we are not to pursue an "experience" of the Holy Spirit. We are, instead, to pursue intimacy and authenticity with our Heavenly Father and remain expectantly open to how He chooses to use and empower us.

Spirit Translocation

So, for the purposes of discussing spirit travel, my belief is that the Apostle John did, in fact, experience spirit travel as accounted in Revelation 4:1,2. John tells us that as he looked up into the sky, he saw a door opened in heaven, and he was called up to it. As soon as he heard the voice, he tells us that he was "in the Spirit" and was now up in heaven, observing everything the Spirit of God wanted him to document. Later, in Chapter 21, he again asserts that he was "carried away in the Spirit to a great and high mountain..." Ezekiel tells us that he experienced the same thing![108]

John was deep in meditation on the Lord when Jesus Himself appeared to John. He fell on his face in terror when he saw Jesus. Why was he so terrified? It was logically because Jesus appeared in glory, and not as the man that John had known. My belief that this was not simply a vision is based on the intense fear that John experienced. Generally speaking, when people in the Bible experienced visions, even prophetic visions with all their bizarre metaphors, the response was not terror. I believe John had a literal encounter with Jesus that day and that Jesus invited John to join Him in Heaven for a momentary glimpse at God's kingdom and plans, unfettered by space and time.

---

[108] Ezekiel 3:14

Astral Projection
Webster's dictionary defines astral projection as the act of separating the spirit or consciousness from the physical body. It is further clarified as an intentional act of having the spirit leaving the body, whereas an out-of-body experience happens involuntarily, such as in a near-death experience.

Certain pagan practitioners of astral projection use Ecclesiastes 12:6,7, which speaks of a "silver cord," to say the Bible endorses this idea. The "silver cord" is used biblically to describe the connection between body and spirit. Once the cord is severed, figuratively speaking, the person dies. This cord is not, however, a "tether" that one can use to anchor his soul to his body so he can have many happy returns.

Resurrection vs. Animation

It is said that Satan does not have the power to create, only to imitate. This idea is certainly challenged by the magicians in Egypt turning their rods into snakes. After all, Satan did *create* rebellion, didn't he? What is probably more accurate is that the enemy cannot create new spirits or resurrect a spirit back into a body. So, when it comes to resurrection, only God has and can grant the power to bring someone back to life. The enemy's best tactic is animation, or the ability to bring "life" to inanimate objects. Bear in mind that the common theme in these examples of resurrection is the glorification of God.

Resurrection
Jesus raised people from the dead. Peter raised people from the dead. Elijah raised people from the dead. We see many examples throughout the Scriptures of people that are resurrected. In Elijah's case, a woman believed in the word of the Lord.[109] In Peter's case, many believed in the Lord as a result.[110] Once again, the miraculous is intended to draw people to God.

Animation
The enemy, through the means of magic, brought to life the staffs of the Egyptian wise men, sorcerers and magicians.[111] We read in Revelation 13:15 that he will also "give breath to the image of the beast" so that it will speak and appear alive. The father of lies, Satan himself, is in the

---

[109] 1 Kings 17:17-24

[110] Acts 9:36-42

[111] Exodus 7:10-12

business of deception. All of the counterfeits we have discussed so far are designed to deceive, and animation is no exception. Both of the above scripture references reinforce this fact.

Divine dictation vs. Automatic writing

The concept of a message from God is well chronicled throughout Scripture, and has been covered, in part, in previous chapters. Divine dictation is not much different, and could probably be easily lumped in under Prophecy, Word of Wisdom or Word of Knowledge. We have identified it separately in response to an obvious counterfeit that needed to be identified as such.

Divine Dictation
God has communicated with His children throughout the ages in many ways, one of which is the dictating of a specific message. This is how we came to have the Scriptures. King David describes this happening to himself. "All this," said David, "the LORD made me understand in writing by His hand upon me, all the details of this pattern" 1 Chr. 28:11-19. John describes something similar in Revelation 14:13 where he is also instructed what to write.

Automatic Writing
Whether hypnosis based or occult based, the pattern of automatic writing is the same. A person is to "free" themselves from conscious thought and make a deliberate effort to write subconsciously, essentially writing with no thought as to the words or content. Some write this off as silly and nonsensical, while freeing, but others practice this art in an effort to allow an outside force to take them over and dictate through them, typically in a trance state.

Mark of God vs. Mark of the beast

"Marking" is symbolic of ownership. Biblically, it implies agreement with, or submission under, an authority. In some cases, the marking is metaphorical, in other cases, it is literal. In some cases it is participatory, in other cases, it is one-directional. In any case, having the mark, or the lack thereof, generally is a matter of life and death.

Mark of God
God marks His people. He marked those of the children of Israel that lamented the abominations of their countrymen.[112] He marked Cain in

---

[112] Ezekiel 9:1-6

order to protect him from being murdered.[113] He also instructed the Israelites to mark their doorposts in order to protect them from the angel of death.[114]

Here we see three different instances of God's protective mark. In the first case, it is God initiated, in the second case, God responds to Cain's lament of fear and marks him, and in the third case, God instructs His people to mark their homes in order to be under His protection.

Additionally, there seem to be different types of markings. In the first case, from Ezekiel, the marking is symbolic, as Ezekiel is having a vision. In the case of Cain, we assume the mark to be physical, as it is designed to protect him from attack from other people. Of course, in the case of the angel of death, the blood on the doorposts was a metaphorical act designed to protect in the unique crossing of the spiritual plane with the physical.

Mark of the beast
The mark of the beast[115] is an element of the end times that causes much speculation among Christians. There is much intrigue over what the mark of the beast will be, and over how literal it will be. Will it be a UPC code? Will it be a microchip? We will simply need to watch and be wary, that we are not deceived if we are to encounter such a moment in history.

Ministry of the Holy Spirit vs. Sorcery

It is no doubt that this comparison seems disjointed at first glance, especially for those of us that do not know much about the Ministry of the Holy Spirit or witchcraft.

Ministry of the Holy Spirit
This terminology is no official label; it is simply a moniker for reference's sake. What we are describing here is the work of the Holy Spirit in the context of affirming and unifying the Body of Christ, as referenced in the scripture, "Again I say to you, that if two of you agree on earth about anything that they may ask, it shall be done for them by My Father who is in heaven. For where two or three have gathered together in My name, I am there in their midst." Matthew 18:20

---

[113] Genesis 4:13-16

[114] Exodus 12:7, 12-13

[115] Revelation 14:9-11

God promises to join His children when we gather for His purpose, in agreement with His desires. He does so through the Holy Spirit. When we join together as Christians for the purpose of fellowship or ministering to one another, the Holy Spirit inspires, prompts, and enables our gifts so all the members of the body can perform their ordained roles, as spelled out in Ephesians 4.

As a group begins to pray for a specific person or situation, it is common for some people to receive confirming scripture, for others to receive a word of wisdom, for others to discern any opposition from the enemy, and still others to be filled with mercy, as a way of relating to the person in need. There are countless other ways that the Spirit employs brothers and sisters in Christ to minister to each other. Desiree and I have had the privilege of experiencing the Ministry of the Holy Spirit as a regular part of the separate ministries that we are part of.

Why does the Spirit do this? Well, quite simply, it is because we are the Church. If church is not a building or a destination, but rather the sum of the children of God, then we are the Church, and we each have a role and gifting for the operation and stewardship of His Church. I can guarantee you that these times of fellowship and ministry are the most encouraging, unifying and intimate times we ever experience with other believers, because that is what we were designed for! As the early church experienced in Acts 4:31-32, "When they had prayed, the place where they had gathered together was shaken, and they were all filled with the Holy Spirit and began to speak the word of God with boldness. And the congregation of those who believed were of one heart and soul…"

This, brothers and sisters, is how the Church, how we, were designed to engage with each other. Does this mean that every single time we partake of the Ministry of the Holy Spirit, we experience signs and wonders? No, there are plenty of times when the work of the Spirit is more subtle-undeniable still, but subtle.

Sorcery
Once again, the enemy has a counterfeit for the work of the Spirit. Witchcraft and sorcery are interchangeably translated these days from the Greek work *pharmakeia*, where our modern word "pharmacy" comes from. In the context of witchcraft and sorcery, the use of mind-altering herbs, toxins and potions has historically been associated with enabling a practitioner to connect with the spirit realm. While deliberate employ of drugs and hallucinogens for this purpose is surely outweighed by recreational drug use, the end result is the same; drug use facilitates demonic influence.

A friend of mine, "Rob," recently shared with me a story from his past. Before coming to salvation, Rob had fallen deep into a cocaine addiction, and as he was part of a distribution channel, he had access to lots of it. He related with me that as he was in the climax of the "high," he started hearing voices. The voices were very strong, and their message was clear. As the high would quickly start to wear off, the voices would fade with it. Rob had a couple of friends that he would get high with, and he clearly remembers that the voices started telling him that one friend, "Mike," was the anti-Christ. At first, he just shrugged it off, but over the course of a few months, the message became stronger and stronger. "Mike is the anti-Christ; you have to save the world!" The demonic influence was getting more powerful, and Rob was starting to take it quite seriously. He began to believe that he would need to kill Mike. One day, the three friends got high together. As the high set in, Rob heard the voices again, and it was clear that this was the time to take action. As he was considering how to proceed, Mike spoke up. "Go ahead, Rob, just do it." Rob looked at him and inquired, "What are you talking about?" Mike replied, "I know I'm the anti-Christ. It's okay, I'm ready. Just do it quickly." It was about this time that the high began wearing off and they started returning to their senses.

There is more to this story, but we'll stop here. Praise be to God, Mike was spared, and Rob has been amazingly transformed through the power of the Holy Spirit.

Just as the Holy Spirit works through the hearts of independent people, delivering to each one individually and uniquely a confirming message for the purpose of ministry, fellowship and ultimately, the delight of the Father, so the enemy works between unbelievers to bring a corroborating and cohesive message to destruction.

Mazzaroth vs. Zodiac

Mazzaroth (Constellations)
Once again, we see God's original design distorted and re-appropriated for occultic purposes. The mazzaroth is the original depiction of the constellations. God is challenging Job, and using His created works to prove His point. "Can you bind the cluster of the Pleiades, or loose the belt of Orion? Can you bring out Mazzaroth in its season? Or can you guide the Great Bear with its cubs? Do you know the ordinances of the heavens? Can you set their dominion over the earth? Job 38:31-33

God made the stars and constellations to, in part, be signs to us for His divine purpose. The stations bear the same names today as they did millennia ago, and as we are told in Romans 1:20, His purpose in creation is to represent His invisible attributes through visual stimuli.

Zodiac

The Chaldeans of the Bible were known for the corruption of God's design for the stars. They became the masters of astrology, adopting the stellar symbols and movements and using them for divination. Of course, astrology is just as prevalent today as it ever has been. Countless people, including some people who claim Jesus as their Savior, scour the newspaper for reassurance from the horoscope. What does God have to say about this?

Of course, God knew that His invisible attributes would be ignored and distorted. He knew people would suppress the truth, even though His design is so evident. We are cautioned that people would become futile in their speculations, and that their foolish hearts would be darkened.[116] That seems like a fitting description of those under the influence of the zodiac.

Conclusion

The enemy would have us stay intimidated and fearful of his treachery. He will use every opportunity to deceive and influence, and if previous chapters have highlighted some of the subtle ways he deceives, then this chapter has highlighted some of the more aggressive, occultic ways he mimics the working of the Holy Spirit. If previous chapters illuminate the ways he deceives believers, then this chapter may more specifically identify some of the ways he intimidates believers. Fear and confusion are good ways to paralyze a Christian, and some of these topics are good tools to that end.

Remember that the Creator of the universe indwells His children: those who have surrendered their hearts to Him, repented of their sin, and believed on the work that Jesus Christ did in paying our punishment on the cross and rising from the dead to bring us new life. And, as Scripture states in Romans 8:11, the same Spirit that raised Jesus from the dead dwells in us. We must live like we believe this truth; "Greater is He who is within you than he who is in the world."

---

[116] Romans 1:18-25

CHAPTER 12

AUTHENTIC VS. COUNTERFEIT: SUPER-HUMAN ABILITY

"I believe that God likes to do astounding things through His children. I want to be ready if He chooses to do so through me."

One of my favorite movies is the M. Night Shamalan movie starring Bruce Willis, "Unbreakable." It chronicles the journey of a man into his place in destiny as a hero. Samuel Jackson's character, Mr. Glass, helps propel the emerging hero through his awakening process. Mr. Glass has a theory. He believes that comic books are a modern way of maintaining true stories of legend, and that these comic books, while they become an exaggeration of reality, reflect actual occurrences in the battle between good and evil.

Based on all the descriptions of how God has used regular people to demonstrate His power, triumph over evil, restore justice, and change the world, we could build a tongue-in-cheek case for how comic books are really written about heroes of the faith: children of God who, in alignment with and in the authority of the Holy Spirit, did remarkable things for the glory of God.

However, just mentioning the term "super-human ability" will make many Christians cringe, as the thought denotes an intrinsic "specialness" about an individual. However, as we examine some biblical examples of super-human acts, we will see that once again it is the Spirit that empowers. In some cases, we see counterfeits, while in others, we do not. Why are these people enabled with such extraordinary abilities?

Let's begin with an example from the life of Elijah.

Super Speed

According to a story from 1 Kings 18, the prophet Elijah outran King Ahab's chariot. Elijah started from Mount Carmel and ran all the way to Jezreel. It was a distance of approximately 26 miles. In other words, Elijah basically ran a marathon in a robe and sandals against a horse and chariot.[117] And Elijah won.

Who was Elijah? Elijah was a prophet of God. Prophets of the Old Testament played a significant role opposite the kings of Israel and

---

[117] 1 Kings 18:44-46

Judah. The ancient prophets are nowadays thought of as "checks and balances" to the kings: their divine authority to the royal authority. They shouldn't have been needed; kings were anointed by God. Kings should have been up to the task of spiritual leadership over God's people. But, we all know the sordid stories of so many of the kings, leading (or following) their people into idolatry and wickedness. The prophets, as in the case with Elijah, were God's mouthpiece to the king, whether the king wanted to hear them or not.

Elijah had just killed the prophets of Baal. He had called fire from heaven and trounced the idolatrous leadership of the nation. Jezebel, the wicked queen, was not present. She was back at home awaiting her husband, King Ahab. Why did God empower Elijah to make this run? Some believe that Elijah wanted to tell Jezebel in person about how he defeated her pagan prophets, but the Scriptures do not elaborate on the actual reason.

Regarding counterfeits of "super-speed," we do not see any direct ones in scripture, but based on the other categories where the enemy has copied the authentic act, it would not surprise me to learn of such instances in the modern day.

Super Strength

Divine Strength
Samson discovered his super-strength quite by accident. A lion ran toward him to attack, and he tore it apart like it was a loaf of bread (my metaphor).[118] After that, he experienced many, many more moments of might under the influence of the Spirit of God. In every case, it is reported that "the Spirit of the LORD came upon him mightily."

Who was Samson? He was a judge of Israel. According to Judges 15:20, he ruled for twenty years, at a time when the Philistines were oppressors of Israel. God marked him, before his birth, for a very special purpose. His purpose seemed to be intricately tied to the liberation of Israel from the Philistines, for even when he broke with tradition and pursued a Philistine woman, the Scriptures record this detail, "...it was of the LORD, for He was seeking an occasion against the Philistines. Now at that time the Philistines were ruling over Israel." Judges 14:4

The Spirit of God empowered Samson in an unusual way when compared to other characters in the Bible. He had an agreement with

---

[118] Judges 14:5,6

God, in essence; he was to never drink wine, never cut his hair, and never touch a dead body, and in return, he would have unimaginable strength. He had a part to play, and when he breached the "contract," so to speak, the Spirit did not empower him. Once his hair had been cut off, the super-strength left him, and he was captured and blinded. And, once Samson's hair had grown back, in one last hurrah, Samson called on the Lord, asking Him for one last burst of strength. We all know the story; Samson pushes apart the pillars of the building where he was entertaining his enemies, and the resulting collapse kills more Philistines in his death than he killed during his lifetime.

Demonic Strength
"...and he had his dwelling among the tombs. And no one was able to bind him anymore, even with a chain; because he had often been bound with shackles and chains, and the chains had been torn apart by him and the shackles broken in pieces, and no one was strong enough to subdue him." Mark 5:3,4

"And the man, in whom was the evil spirit, leaped on them and subdued all of them and overpowered them, so that they fled out of that house naked and wounded." Acts 19:16

When we think of the hallucinogenic drug, PCP, we commonly associate it with stories of super-human strength. The drug's effect on the body dramatically increases a person's ability to exert strength, as well as to decrease the awareness of pain. I have heard stories of PCP users breaking sinks off of walls and throwing them and others overturning cars. While we could certainly attribute this strength to the chemical properties of the drug itself, we can also recall the fact that the enemy capitalizes on the "impaired state" that drug users choose to enter.

Flight

Flight (Physical transport by the Holy Spirit)
In the Scriptures we see reference to the Holy Spirit transporting people. The reasons are varied; Enoch[119] and Elijah[120] are brought to heaven, while Philip[121] is taken to a different city to minister there.

---

[119] Hebrews 11:5

[120] 2 Kings 2:11,12

[121] Acts 8:35-40

Who were these men? Enoch was a man that was pleasing to God. Elijah was a prophet of Israel. And Philip was an apostle in the early church. What do all three of these men have in common? They all had divine appointments: two were to bypass death and meet God, and one was scheduled to preach the gospel at Azotus and onward to Caesarea.

Levitation (Transport by demonic force)
What we typically think of in regards to levitation is the picture of a New-Age practitioner of Transcendental Meditation, legs folded, bouncing his way across a padded mat, all in a bliss-like state. This doesn't present a very convincing case for the logical mind. However, we have also heard accounts from the mission field where people, clearly under demonic influence, have flown.

We see in scripture, during the great temptation of Jesus, how Satan transported Jesus. This is not a figment of Jesus's imagination, it is real; Satan tries to tempt Jesus to "prove" Himself by throwing Himself off the roof of the temple, putting Himself in harm's way.[122]

Why would the devil need to "fly" Jesus to the mountaintop or the pinnacle of the temple? One explanation is that Satan is not omniscient, nor is he free from the space-time continuum, and at that place in history, he would not have had all the details of Jesus' plan of redemption. It is said that perhaps he was trying to "size-up" Jesus, not being privy to the nature of this incarnate revelation of God on earth. Perhaps Satan was trying to impress Jesus, maybe he wanted to intimidate Him.

Could Jesus fly? Of course He could, in the power of the Spirit of God. He did it more than once, both in the Old Testament as the angel of the LORD,[123] as well as in the New Testament as Jesus Christ, when He ascended to the Father.[124]

Conclusion

To summarize this look at "super-human" ability, we must put it all in context of God's purpose. Every miracle was always intended to bring God glory. What does that mean? It means one of two things: the fame of God's intervention spreads through the community and people praise God as a direct result, or, God intervenes for His own good pleasure.

---

[122] Matthew 4:5-9

[123] Judges 13:19-22

[124] Luke 24:51

As we stated at the beginning of this book, we are simply compiling stories of the Holy Spirit's activity from the Scriptures. Why are we doing this? The purpose is twofold: it is to reveal to the Evangelical Christian the rich nature of the work of the Holy Spirit for the encouragement and inspiration of His people, and it is to put the work of the enemy in its rightful place, as a cheap knockoff of the amazing and creative work of God.

In speaking of "super-human" ability, we do not mean to trivialize the work of the Holy Spirit or make light of it. We only desire to examine every characteristic the Bible records about the Spirit's activity, so that Christians will view the Spirit of God with the respect and reverence that He is due. It is high time that we stop being awestruck at the enemy's show of force, and start being engrossed with the unexplainable power, authority, benevolence and creativity of the Holy Spirit.

How does this same Spirit of God manifest in your life and in mine? It would be one thing to look at the examples from this chapter, smile and nod, and relegate these super-human experiences to God's archaic and random way of empowering people this way. Yet, we must remember the case of Samson, who wielded his strength in his anger. He acted rashly and violently, and yet, the Spirit of God was upon him and he led the people of God in strength. Are we living in a way that expects God to show up in an amazing way? We know what Jesus likes in this context, He loves it when people step out in faith. A man's friends tear a hole in a roof and lower him down to where Jesus was teaching, blocked by the crowds. Jesus sees their faith in action and heals their friend (Mark 2:5). Jesus tells the heathen centurion, "Go, it shall be done for you as you have believed." He praises the man and tells everyone within earshot, "Truly I say to you, I have not found such great faith with anyone in Israel. (Matt.8:10-13).

Jesus includes us in this great potential when He tells us, "...for truly I say to you, if you have faith the size of a mustard seed, you will say to this mountain, 'Move from here to there,' and it will move; and nothing will be impossible to you." Matthew 17:20

The problem these days is not with the Holy Spirit, it is with us! He tells us that nothing will be impossible to us! The stories we have examined throughout this chapter should not be dismissed as lore-rather, they should serve as an inspiration to us of what the possibilities are for a child of God who is abiding in Jesus, yielded to the Father, and completely expectant of the work of the Holy Spirit within us.

CHAPTER 13

THE CREATIVITY OF THE SPIRIT OF GOD

"The fact that the Spirit of God inspires creativity and ingenuity moves me to join Him and open myself to Him, for His employment."

The Holy Spirit is beyond our summations. We may try to categorize the divine, but as surely as we do, our imaginations begin to limit us. In our ponderings on the Spirit, there are bound to be aspects of His character that we overlook. In this chapter, we will look at what the Scriptures teach us about the creative nature of God, through His Spirit. The Holy Spirit is a creative entity, and His handiwork displays His inspiration. There are many, many ways He uses His creativity.

A look back a human history gives us glimpses of creative advances, many of which we take for granted today. Some of the advances seem as old as humanity itself, so we tend to attribute them to some long process of trial and error, with mankind being the ultimate victor and human intellect the fuel to such ingenuity. But, I believe that many of these advances in technology and artisanship are the direct result of the Holy Spirit's influence.

The Scriptures speak of Jabal and his brother and Jubal, and their half-brother Tubal-cain. Jabal is credited as being the *father of nomadic ranchers*, while Jubal is called the *father of musicians of stringed and wind instruments*, and finally, Tubal-cain is termed the *father of welding*.[125]

I don't know about you, but when I read about these people, I have to ask the question, "How did these men figure this stuff out?" How does a man figure out how to invent brand new musical instruments? In the case of the lyre, how did he learn to calibrate string for the different notes of the lyre? How did he figure out what material would make good musical string?

As for Tubal-cain, how did he determine that he could chip out of rock a metal that could be melted at extremely high heat and hammered and folded and shaped to create tools and weapons?

As far as Jabal goes, I would assume that being a rancher would be relatively easy to figure out, but since wealth in those days was

---

[125] Genesis 4:19-22

measured by how much livestock you owned, an intimate understanding of animal husbandry would be critical to creating wealth through the breeding of animals.

Where did these people learn such amazing creative skills?

The simple answer is that the Holy Spirit enabled these people with this creativity and ingenuity. This shouldn't be too hard to accept-after all, the very first mention of the Trinity, the plural God, *Elohim*, in the very first verse in the Bible, states that God *created* the heavens and the earth. He went on to make us in His image; He made us creative, among other things. One of the tasks He gave Adam was creative, to name all the animals He had created.

In Craftsmanship

As we proceed through the Bible, there are many accounts of how the Spirit of God inspired and filled people to be creative, and generally speaking, for a specific cause. In the tabernacle's design specifications from Exodus 28, God calls on gifted artisans to create the garments and accouterments of the high priest. This is a complex outfit that will likely require a weaver, a tailor, a metal worker, and a jeweler.

The work described is very specific, very delicate, and very much designed by God's specifications in order to point to a coming Redeemer. From the specified colors to the materials used, it all points prophetically to the last High Priest that God would ordain, God in the flesh, Jesus Christ. The precision and purity of the construction and use of the holy garments illustrates mankind's position before a perfect God and His provision for our approach to His presence. It is all designed to point to our salvation from hell and reconciliation with the Father.

Of course, this is not the only place in Scripture where we see God's deliberate design and empowerment. In Exodus 31, God enables other people: a carpenter, a farmer, and a perfumer. God tells Moses who to assign the work to-a man named Bezalel. He tells Moses that He has filled him with "The Spirit of God in wisdom, in understanding, in knowledge, and in all kinds of craftsmanship" that include artwork of gold, silver, and bronze and in cutting diamonds and precious stones, and in wood carving. Wow! That is a lot of "natural" talent! God then tells Moses that He has also appointed other artisans to create the tabernacle tent, the tables and candelabra, the ark of the covenant, the altars, priestly garments, the anointing oil, the incense and every other item on God's design list.

Again, the critical element here is not simply that these people were supernaturally creative. The important thing was for them to respond to God's invitation to join Him in His design and His agenda.

In Poetry

The Holy Spirit is creative. He inspires and empowers people in various artistic manners. A friend of ours recently shared how, though she has written poetry her whole life, the Lord has started giving her poetry in her prayer times. He will give her line after line until He is finished. Sometimes it is a little treasure just for her. Other times it is meant to minister to someone else.

A missionary to the Philippines in the 1930s, Frank Laubach, kept a journal in which he chronicled his immersion into prayer and communing with the Father. In the tradition of Brother Lawrence's "The Practice of the Presence of God," he began a journey to remain in communion with the Father for increasingly longer time spans during the day. During the deepest time in his journaling, he recounts the following:

> May 24, 1930 - *Souls dead to God look sadly out of hungry eyes*
>
> This has been a week of wonders. God is at work *everywhere* preparing the way for his work in Lanao. I shall tell you some of the wonders presently. But just at this moment you must hear more of this sacred evening. The day had been rich but strenuous, so I climbed "Signal Hill" back of my house talking and listening to God all the way up, all the way back, all the lovely half hour on the top. And God talked back! I let my tongue go loose and from it there flowed poetry far more beautiful than any I ever composed. It flowed without pausing and without ever a failing syllable for a half hour. I listened astonished and full of joy and gratitude. I wanted a Dictaphone for I knew that I should not be able to remember it-and now I cannot. "Why," someone may ask, "did God waste his poetry on you alone, when you could not carry it home." You will have to ask God that question. I only know He did and I am happy in the memory.[126]

We know that significant sections of the Old Testament were written as poetry. God loves to create poetry and bless His children with it. I myself have been writing poetry as long as I can remember. And, like most *creatives* out there, I have always created out of my own inspiration and

---

[126] "Letters by a Modern Mystic," by Frank Laubach

motivation. But, in the last couple of years, I have begun to pray through specific works I am writing, asking for the Holy Spirit to lead me at every word and every thought. At this point, it is actually a lot harder for me than just writing out of my own intellect. It is a constant effort to keep myself out of His way as I await His prompting and inspiration.

In Writing

A remarkable woman, known nowadays simply as Madame Guyon, was a woman completely set apart for God. She suffered, at the hands of the Catholic Church, persecution for her strange devotion to the Father. Her intimacy with God was such that it didn't fit the dogma of their system, and they chastened her out of fear. In her autobiography, she recounts the following manner that the Spirit enabled her to write:

> I still continued to write, and with incredible quickness, for the hand could hardly follow the spirit which dictated, and during this long work I did not change my conduct, nor make use of any book. The copyist could not, however diligent, copy in five days what I wrote in a single night. What is good in it comes from you alone, O my God...For he made me stop writing when I had time to write and I could conveniently do it, and when I seemed to have a very great need of sleeping, it was then that he made me write. When I wrote by day there were continual interruptions, and had not time to eat, owing to the number who used to come. I had to give up everything as soon as it was asked for, and in addition I had the maid who served me in the state of which I have spoken, and she without cause used to come and suddenly interrupt me, according as her whim took her. I often left the meaning half finished, without troubling myself whether what I was writing was connected or not. The places which may be defective are so only because sometimes I wished to write as I had the time and then it was not grace at its fountainhead. If these passages were numerous it would be pitiable. At last I accustomed myself to follow God in his way, not in mine.[127]

In Music

In a Biblical account, we see Moses lead the children of Israel in song. Exodus 15:1 states, "Then Moses and the sons of Israel sang this song

---

[127] "Autobiography of Madame Guyon," by Jeanne Marie Bouvier de La Motte Guyon

to the LORD, and said, 'I will sing to the LORD, for He is highly exalted; the horse and its rider He has hurled into the sea...'"

I believe that we must credit this inspiration to create a song of praise to the Spirit of God. It was not an existing song; it related directly to the deliverance God had just performed. It is human nature, of course, to doubt the Spirit's inspiration of Moses' song, and credit it to Moses' gratitude alone. However, this was apparently not the only time that Moses was inspired by the Spirit to craft a song of praise, as we see in Deuteronomy 31. Revelation 15:3 describes how, in heaven, *overcomers* will sing the "Song of Moses, the bond-servant of God, and the song of the Lamb..." Moses' song is called the Lamb's song-could its inspiration be any clearer?

A dear friend, whom I will call Jim, is passionate about music, and has spent a considerable amount of time as a "worship leader" in the church. As I also spent many years playing music in church, we struck up a conversation about the expectations of a worship leader, both from the congregation and from his own motivations. We both agreed that there is a pressure to deliver not only a musically excellent performance, but also to lead God's people into a worshipful time of singing praise to Him. Inevitably, worship leaders end up trying to manipulate the setting, the Sunday morning environment, in order to set a "mood" for worship, thereby making it conducive for the congregation to join in.

Isn't it obvious when worship leaders do this? We might dim the lights during a poignant moment in the service, or we may ask people to stand/sit/kneel to "draw in" the audience. We may strum softly while we pray, and, if we really go out on a limb, we may even let people know when it would be good to "lift up holy hands" during worship. All of this is, of course, human motivation inspired by human expectation. And, while it may appear to work sometimes, it usually is pretty transparent, leaving some people with a distaste for the disingenuous nature of the service, and others with a manufactured experience that leaves them warm and fuzzy, but no closer to experiencing true worship collectively as a church body.

Jim continued to relate to me some of the moments where the Holy Spirit is quite clearly present during worship. In his personal experience, it is when he has been alone with God, and he is simply adoring the Father in song. There have been several moments when the Holy Spirit has filled him briefly with words and melody to play and sing as an offering to God. To Jim, these moments serve as a sobering awareness of the need to lead a congregation in personal worship; for the rest to worship, he must first be worshiping. What does Scripture say about this? We are encouraged to admonish one another with psalms and hymns and spiritual songs,[128] and to be filled with the Spirit, singing and making melody with our hearts to the Lord.[129]

Summary

We have looked at a handful of ways that the Spirit inspires and enables people in creativity: weavers, tailors, jewelers, metal workers, musicians, ranchers, carpenters, farmers, poets and songwriters. How many other categories of artisans are there? How many other ways does a creative God expect us to create with the talents He has given us? Our God is a creative God who has blessed people with creative facets of His own character. We may experience a certain level of skill using these talents under our own employ, but how much more when wielding creativity in the power of the Spirit?

This is really a poignant example of how our natural life is a spiritual life. We are spiritually alive, if Christ Jesus has done a saving and regenerating work within us. If we are spiritually alive, then how is it possible to "turn it off" when we are at work or play, and "turn it on" when we are at Church or engaged in ministry? It doesn't work like that at all! We cannot separate our existence into categories, nor can we assume that Church attendance is the most spiritual part of the week. God wants all of us. He wants every little bit. He wants every moment. And, I can speak from experience when I say that He will undoubtedly use anything and everything in our life to point us back to Him. If we are His workmanship, doesn't it stand to reason that the talents He has given us should be employed to be a witness of Him?

What could the Body of Christ, the Church, look like if we all were to be filled with the Spirit in this manner? How drastically different would we be if we created, not out of our ingenuity and inspiration, but out of the enlightenment of the Spirit of God? As we talked about this very subject, my dad shared these thoughts with me:

> *"The hallmarks of a Spirit filled church flow with this type of thing throughout its every aspect of ministry, worship, and service. It is like reading of the early church in Acts 2. Everything flowed out of the spontaneous personality of Christ in them, but it was only after ten days of abandonment to Him that any of it occurred. Yes, there*

---

[128] Colossians 3:16

[129] Ephesians 5:18,19

are imitations and without a solid foundation in scripture, most folks can't tell the difference. But, those who know the Lord and are filled by Him are not swayed by any of this. They are just busy about their Master's business. Others who feel they are on stage and being observed stumble through events and life trying to appear spiritual when the most spiritual thing they can do is die out to all of it by dying to themselves.

We train our children to behave a certain way, and in public they usually embarrass us to death. They understand a certain behavior under certain conditions, but left to themselves, they always serve themselves until their day of salvation. It is then and there that they begin to understand that He is All and they are nothing and most everything else that they do in the flesh is a misrepresentation of Him. They must die to themselves, the world, and all the flattery that comes with Christianity. Then I think you begin to see the craftsmen, the architects, the preachers and leaders of the Church emerge. They have and produce no agenda of their own, just service to mankind and their Master. They can and do thrive in any culture, any situation, any danger, any ministry-why, because they are filled with and guided by the Spirit of God. This is something we know little of."

We must ask ourselves why God has given us the creative talents we have. Are they simply to pursue a hobby during this life, this short phase of the Kingdom of God? Are they for our amusement and enjoyment alone? I do not believe this to be the case. I have always written out of inspiration, but it has been earthly inspiration. I am still learning to create out of the inspiration of the Holy Spirit. I am still learning how to be "filled with the Spirit" in my area of craftsmanship. What I can say, in my limited experience, is that His creativity through me seems to bring about a spiritual fruit by ministering to someone, and produces praise to God. Works created of my own inspiration serve to only inspire others at best, and seem to produce praise of me instead of God.

Chapter 14

The Boundlessness of the Spirit of God

"The Spirit of God has an agenda that is far beyond my domain. He reminds me that He will use whomever and whatever He wants, however He wants to. Who am I to limit Him?"

As stated before, we Christians are an arrogant bunch. We act like we have got our fingers on the pulse of God. We act like our worth is greater that the worth of other people. I have even witnessed Western Christians portray themselves as "better" than Christians from third-world countries, as if we have God figured out, as evidenced by our affluence. We often forget that God is at work outside of ourselves, and outside of the Church. God, through His Holy Spirit, is active and engaged all throughout His entire Creation.

We fiercely claim God as our own, but in reality, we behave like God is somewhat disinterested or uninvolved in our existence. We generally assume His activity and priority as being intricately tied to what the Church is up to. We are most comfortable keeping God at arms' length and at a safe distance, where He certainly must be obsessing over the administration of the Church.

The children of Israel were no different in their time. They kept their distance from God, always wanting a judge, a king, anybody at all to deal with God on their behalf. Yet, in spite of their insolence, they maintained a possessiveness over God. They wanted all the pride and protection of being His people, without the obedience and requirement that came with it. They wanted the exclusivity of being His chosen, yet, the Scriptures are quite clear; God was also at work in other places and other peoples.

We know that God has command over kings and nations, and anything else He deems useful. The Scriptures tell us that the king's heart is in His hand,[130] and that He exalts kings and tears them down.[131] We know that He creates vessels for honor and others for dishonor.[132] How does this work, if not through the influence of the Holy Spirit?

---

[130] Proverbs 21:1

[131] Daniel 2:21

[132] Romans 9

We know that no one can come to Jesus for salvation unless the Father draws him.[133] This is the work of the Holy Spirit in those that are lost in sin, drawing people unto repentance. This is perhaps the most obvious work of the Spirit of God out in the world. Yet, there are many other ways the Scriptures depict the activity of the Spirit in the world throughout His entire creation.

The Holy Spirit's activity in unbelievers

The Holy Spirit is the source and the fuel of any empowerment of gifts, signs or wonders, and we see several examples in the Scriptures where He actually empowers unbelievers to fulfill His agenda. King Cyrus of Persia prophesies,[134] Cornelius the Roman centurion sees a vision,[135] King Abimelech of Gerar has a dream from God,[136] Hagar the Egyptian hears the voice of God,[137] and God calls Nebuchadnezzar "My servant," as He blesses his kingdom with promises of power and retribution.[138]

Sometimes, God's purpose becomes very clear in hindsight, but sometimes it does not. King Cyrus' prophecy indicated that God wanted him to build a temple in Jerusalem. Cornelius' vision prepared him to receive the Gospel when Peter came to town. Abimelech's dream warned him against taking Sarah as his wife. But, what about Hagar? Why did God interact with her? What about Nebuchadnezzar? Why did God choose to use a pagan king for His purpose? The Scriptures aren't nearly as clear about these cases. And yet, God demonstrates that He is active and powerful, far beyond the borders of our comfort zone. This is just as true today as it was back then.

A friend of ours, who I'll call "John," recently shared with us an experience they had. A friend of John had been in a low place, and struggling with circumstance and depression. John sensed the Lord's prompting to share the gospel with him. This man, ultimately, did not do anything personally with the good news of Jesus Christ. However, this same man received a phone call soon after from yet another friend, Julie,

---

[133] John 6:44

[134] Ezra 1:1-4

[135] Acts 10:3

[136] Genesis 20:1-7

[137] Genesis 21:14-20

[138] Jeremiah 43:10-13

who was struggling with depression, and this unbelieving man shared the gospel with her. After a short time, Julie called him back, elated over the change that Jesus worked in her heart, looking to celebrate with him. The man, of course, did not understand Julie's experience, as he had not received it for himself. But he ultimately, unknowingly, was used as an evangelist for the glory of Jesus Christ.

This is the work of the Holy Spirit in those that are lost in sin: not just drawing people unto repentance, but ultimately, bringing glory to God as He sees fit in the world He created.

The Holy Spirit's activity in Creation

In the Universe
In the beginning God, or *Elohim(the plural God)*, created the heavens and the earth. This clearly involved the Holy Spirit, as the same passage tells us that the Spirit of God was hovering, or vibrating, over the face of the deep.[139] God's design of the cosmos, including this planet, was not just to provide a place for our habitation, but to continually direct our awareness back to Himself as Creator for the express purpose of bringing mankind to Himself. God uses His Creation in several ways; He uses it to draw an immense chasm between His capacity and that of mankind,[140] as in the case of Job. He illustrates how He is in constant care of His earth.[141] He inspires mankind to worship the Creator through the magnificence of what we observe,[142] and finally, He astounds and amazes us when He chooses to bend the rules of the universe through His working of miracles, as in the case of the parting of the Red Sea.[143]

As cliche as we Christians can make such a concept, it does not change the fact of the matter. I like how Rick Warren puts it in "The Purpose Driven Life":

> *"Where is the glory of God? Just look around. Everything created by God reflects his glory in some way. We see it everywhere, from the smallest microscopic form of life to the vast Milky Way, from sunsets and stars to storms and seasons. Creation reveals our Creator's glory. In nature we learn that God is powerful, that he*

---

[139] Genesis 1:1,2

[140] Job 38

[141] Matthew 10:29

[142] Romans 1:19-25

[143] Exodus 14:21

> *enjoys variety, loves beauty, is organized, and is wise and creative. The Bible says, 'The heavens declare the glory of God.*[144]
>
> *Throughout history, God has revealed his glory to people in different settings. He revealed it first in the Garden of Eden, then to Moses, then in the tabernacle and the temple, then through Jesus, and now through the church. It was portrayed as a consuming fire, a cloud, thunder, smoke, and a brilliant light. In heaven, God's glory provides all the light needed."*

In Romans, we see the implication of this truth. God's existence, power and nature are not only seen, but understood by our experience through nature. This is sufficient evidence to lead a person to acknowledging and worshiping the true Creator, our true God.[145] God's supremacy is clearly seen in what He created. But, his attributes are also seen in *how He uses* what He created. The marvel of the burning bush, the spectacle of the Red Sea split open for the exodus, the pillar of cloud and pillar of fire to lead the children of Israel, and the ignition of Elijah's waterlogged altar with fire.

God uses anything and everything He desires to His glory and to His purpose. We know that creation groans for Him.[146] We know that even the rocks would cry out on Jesus' behalf.[147] We know that He created the rainbow as a testimony of His word.[148] His universe is His mouthpiece.

In Animals

Throughout Scripture, God also uses animals for His purpose. We all know the story of flocks of quail being sent daily to the Israelites for their sustenance. We know the story of the plague of frogs in Egypt. We have heard the story where God sent vipers throughout the camp of the Israelites, and we remember the times when Jesus directed vast numbers of fish into Peter's nets. These are all stories where God commands wildlife, but we want to see a bit more personification employed in order to illustrate the work of the Holy Spirit. So, for simplicity's sake, we will look at the most specific examples of God's purpose being achieved through animals.

---

[144] Psalm 19:1

[145] Romans 1:19-25

[146] Romans 8:22

[147] Luke 19:40

[148] Genesis 9:13

God speaks to Balaam through his donkey in order to stop him from proceeding against the will of the Lord.[149] Jonah is swallowed and transported by a great fish in order to bring him into alignment with God's purpose.[150] God provides food to Elijah twice daily during his hiding by having ravens bring him bread and meat.[151]

In "Acts of God"
Jesus calmed the storm and rebuked the wind and rain, and His mastery over the elements astounded the disciples. It is another case involving God's creation and His interaction with it, and the moment serves its purpose as this experience of God in his Creation clearly demonstrates His authority to His disciples.[152] We know that God commands the weather. In figurative language, God's breath creates the ice, and with it He can freeze the ocean. He loads the clouds with moisture and makes them shoot forth lightning. He guides their direction, and uses them to both bring correction and to show His lovingkindness.[153]

The Scriptures speak to God's authority and design of weather, both in a general context and for His specific purpose. God uses violent wind,[154] drought,[155] earthquakes,[156] darkness,[157] tornadoes,[158] floods,[159] and hail,[160] among other things, for judgment as well as for awe and amazement.

---

[149] Numbers 22:25-35

[150] Jonah 1:17, 2:10

[151] 1 Kings 17:1-6

[152] Mark 4:36-41

[153] Job 37:9-13

[154] Ezekiel 13:13

[155] James 5:17,18

[156] Numbers 16:31-33

[157] Isaiah 45:7

[158] 2 Kings 2:1

[159] Genesis 6:17

[160] Exodus 9:22

Conclusion

In Romans 11:22, God reminds us of His character, and the contrast between His goodness and His severity. When we look at Creation, in any capacity, we see the balance of God's attributes. The same insects that are a needed part of the food cycle are the insects that can devastate food crops. The same rain that restores the land can drown it, and the same sunlight that facilitates photosynthesis can scorch the very trees and plants that process it.

I am the LORD, and there is no other, the One forming light and creating darkness, causing well-being and creating calamity; I am the LORD who does all these. Drip down, O heavens, from above, and let the clouds pour down righteousness; Let the earth open up and salvation bear fruit, and righteousness spring up with it. I, the LORD, have created it. Isaiah 45:6-8

God is driving home the point that He is the ultimate, and He is supreme. He makes no apology or reasoning for His action or His design, and He holds in contempt those who question His show of power through Creation. Job also recounts God's disdain for those who would disregard His obvious dominion through the amazing evidence of Creation. Job has questioned God, and God has pushed back. He appears to even pick a fight with Job, in a manner of speaking. He uses two powerful illustrations of creatures that He has engineered, creatures that confound the mind: Behemoth and Leviathan. He throws down the gauntlet at Job to square up and prove to God his accomplishments and his own justification before God.[161]

Job is put squarely in his place before a holy and magnificent Creator as God proves His supremacy through His works, Behemoth and Leviathan. God is using created wonders to astound this human man, once again proving the words of Romans, that God is clearly evident through His works of Creation, and we are without excuse.

And so, we must remember our place before this holy and magnificent God. We must not present ourselves as "high and mighty" before God, as apparently Job had done. And I dare say, that if we proceed each day with eyes and hearts wide open, that we will see His design all around us. Suddenly, we will not be able to go anywhere without constant reminders of the Creator, Elohim. The Spirit of God, the same Spirit that created this earth, will speak to our hearts of God's great design, His intentionality, His thoroughness, His attention to detail, His joy over His creations, and ultimately, His awesome supremacy over all.

---

[161] Job 40-42

Chapter 15

From Skeptic to Believer

"I have come to understand that the Spirit of God is what was missing in my spiritual life. He was there, but my entanglement with the world quenched Him. My disbelief quenched Him. My pride quenched Him. Limiting Him limits me."

In the Star Wars saga, there are two main characters that, while both being "good guys," are quite opposites in how they live out their beliefs. Luke Skywalker and Han Solo are both men who are fighting against the "dark side." The guys I knew always wanted to be like Han Solo. He was a tough guy. He was hard-nosed. I don't know any guys who thought Luke Skywalker was cool.

This analogy holds some interesting implications in our understanding of our journey as a child of God. Han Solo, the cool guy, is the perpetual skeptic. He doesn't believe in "the Force." He only believes in what he can see. He trusts his own instinct, and one of his great skills is out-running the enemy. As such, he chooses to keep a safe distance from any conflict, choosing a weapon that does not require him to engage in hand-to-hand combat: a gun.

> *"Hokey religions and ancient weapons are no match for a good blaster at your side, kid."*
> *-Han Solo*[162]

Luke, on the other hand, is not the cool guy. He seems soft. He is way too interested in this invisible, intangible "Force." He begins his journey as a naïve, immature youth and finishes his journey as a Jedi master. He is introspective. He knows how to be still and contemplative. But, as we see later in his journey, he learns how to stand his ground against an enemy that seems terrifying and undefeatable. He does not run, like the skeptic. He does not avoid conflict with the enemy, like Han Solo. He stands alone, solitary in his defiance to "the dark side," armed with his understanding of "the Force" and a single, hand-held weapon, his light-saber. He goes where the action is, and he engages in hand-to-hand combat.

---

[162] Star Wars: Episode IV-A New Hope, dir. by George Lucas (1977; 20th Century Fox, 2004 dvd).

"Never. I'll never turn to the Dark Side. You've failed, your highness. I am a Jedi, like my father before me."
-Luke Skywalker[163]

Indulge me for a moment in this metaphor. Which character are you? Are you the person who looks good to other people, or are you the person who stands alone in his convictions? Are you the skeptic or the believer? Do you run from the enemy, or do you stand your ground in the boldness of the Spirit?

Our Christianity, at its inception, was much more ethereal than the superstructure that we know it to be today. When Christianity was still a movement, people simply lived and moved in the power of the Spirit. I am not just talking about the disciples-turned-apostles. Many people outside of that title were filled with the Spirit who enabled them to do amazing things within His agenda. We have looked at many such examples throughout this book. The same is true today. Christians all over the world are discovering that God fills, enables and empowers us when we are all about "His business."

This, of course, is not where our journey begins as Christians. Our journey begins with us still very self-centered, focused on the pleasures of life, while the foundations of Biblical knowledge are slowly built in our hearts. At some point, the foundational understandings and behaviors will begin to lose their their fruitfulness in our lives. What used to "work" just won't work any longer. This is our signal that it is time to transition into the next stage of spiritual maturity. This is nothing new. In fact, the author of the book of Hebrews spelled it out for us nearly two thousand years ago.

"Therefore *leaving the elementary teaching* about the Christ, *let us press on to maturity*, not laying again a foundation of repentance from dead works and of faith toward God, of instruction about washings and laying on of hands, and the resurrection of the dead and eternal judgment" Hebrews 6:1-2

It is difficult to leave the foundational doctrines behind us, but Hebrews 6 tells us it is necessary. It is time for us to leave behind the elementary teachings that were our schoolmaster, and move forward into more advanced training as the mature men and women our Father destined us to be.

---

[163] Star Wars: Episode VI-Return of the Jedi, dir. by Richard Marquand (1983; 20th Century Fox, 2006 dvd).

At times, our training in the Spirit is difficult. It can be painful. It can be so hard to anticipate where the training is leading us. It is especially difficult because it takes us off the smooth asphalt highway of our foundational, black and white knowledge, and it leads us off road, into seemingly uncharted pathways, obstructed with overgrowth and pitted with mudholes and obstacles. It is our natural tendency to want to turn back to the solid highway with unobstructed views.

Yet, in proceeding where the pavement ends, this is where our journey into maturity continues. It is truly about the journey. As we push past the overgrowth, we will inevitably confront our own perspectives, as the Lord works to help us see things the way that He does. In other words, you may have your "Peter moment." Remember the story of Peter's vision? God instructed him to eat "unclean" animals. This was obviously in conflict with Peter's Jewish customs. It contradicted what he *knew* was pleasing to God. In this vision, God *seemed* to be contradicting Himself by telling Peter to eat the very food he wasn't allowed to. We know how the story goes, God ultimately sent Peter to the Gentiles to spread the news of Jesus Christ. God used Peter in astounding ways in the early Church. But, Peter first had to journey through some of these difficult moments, this vision in particular being a trial of his faith.

You may encounter similar moments in your journey. You may need wise counsel. You may need another believer who can help interpret what the Lord is trying to impart to you. You may have significant struggles as you transition from the building blocks of faith to the deeper aspects of intimacy and abiding in Christ.

When you do emerge into a mature believer, you will then be tested in your willingness to yield to the Father. And finally, authority will follow this yieldedness. With yieldedness and authority come the outpouring of His Spirit, and when His Spirit flows through you, you will experience God enabling and inspiring you to do things clearly beyond your own abilities. This is the life heroic. This is how our heroes of the faith lived out their destiny.

Heroes of the Faith

As children daydream of being superheroes or Jedi knights, they are feeding a God-designed thirst for action, for influence, and for a "good fight" to wage. I believe we can, and should, help Christians understand the potential of a life in Christ, paint a vision of the future to them, and inspire the Church on to its God-designed place in destiny. However, we need modern day heroes. People are not so much inspired by characters of the past, because we can't relate with them. We have a hard time identifying with Paul, Peter and Phillip. However, there are certainly many, many figures in the faith since then that have lived in the power of the Holy Spirit.

Consider Smith Wigglesworth, who daily lived his calling and healed countless people in astounding ways. Wigglesworth's philosophy was simple, "Before God could bring me to this place (that of working miracles), He had to break me a thousand times. Until God has mowed you down, you will never have this long-suffering (compassion) for others." [164]

Ah! Therein lies the problem. We do not want to be broken, and certainly not more than once. We do not want pain and we do not want to be stripped bare. Yet, the reality is that this happens to us anyway, doesn't it? Life itself takes us through such times-they are guaranteed in one form or another! If we are honest with ourselves, with our children, and with people under our care, discipling, or mentoring, we will present the reality of pain and brokenness so that others can expect it, recognize it, and not waste the opportunity when it comes! An active part of my and Desiree's life, as well as our counseling and mentoring is this very concept; we encourage people to "embrace" the rock-bottom place, the depths of pain, as a time and place to abandon ourselves completely to the Heavenly Father.

Authority requires yielding, and power requires pain, just as a rite of passage requires initiation. This is not a foreign concept to cultures that still practice such rites of passage. It is understood that there will be some level of suffering in order to transition into maturity and receive all the privilege, responsibility and authority that comes with it. Our children need rites of passage, just as children in the faith need them to transition into spiritual adolescence, and finally into maturity, spiritual fatherhood and motherhood, with all the privilege, responsibility and authority that comes with it. Again, to quote Smith Wigglesworth, "There is nothing worth having that you do not have to pay for, either temporally or spiritually."

The Call

The Holy Spirit works in us to inspire, prompt, initiate, and stir up. Is this happening in your heart as His design becomes clearer? If you hope for little, you will receive little. If you dream big, then you will be open to much greater opportunity, if for any reason, than you believe it is possible!

---

[164] "Smith Wigglesworth on Healing," by Smith Wigglesworth

We have taken a cursory look at the activity of the Holy Spirit throughout the Bible. We have examined the Old Testament and the New, and the reality is that we cannot contain the Holy Spirit. We cannot "sum up" the work of the Spirit as being primarily focused on "gifting." We must stop avoiding the Holy Spirit. We evangelicals tend to view the activity of the Spirit in two extreme manifestations: on one hand, we ignore "Him" as a "silent partner" in the Trinity; on the other hand, we hear fantastical stories from the mission field, and we dismiss "Him" still, as we limit that demonstration of power to "primitive" peoples whose superstition demands a requisite manifestation of the Holy Spirit.

Are you apathetic to all this? Does this not ignite a longing in you for life as God designed it? Are you fearful? Do you retreat at the thought of this destiny? Are you filled with doubt? Do you question your adequacy for this task? If so, you are being controlled by lies. Lies, among other things, are messages from the enemy to keep you neutralized, to keep you from realizing your potential in the Lord, and pursuing it.

We will bring this book to a close with the statement we began with: the enemy's greatest triumph against the Church may well be in keeping believers oblivious to and afraid of their potential in Christ Jesus. He only needs to whisper skewed ideas in our ear, and we can be distracted enough to miss God's best. How do we move past the lies? Sit with your Heavenly Father, and ask Him to illuminate a lie that you are believing. Ask for His truth; ask for Scripture to replace that lie. Spend time dissecting this truth and meditating on it with Him.

If you want to live life to the potential God designed you for, then He will certainly take you through the process to prepare you for the authority and calling He has reserved for you. Of course, you can choose to terminate the process and return back to "safe" Christianity. You can choose to continue "clocking in" to your faith, methodically, dutifully, and worse yet, pitifully, and bypass the detour that will take you into your destiny.

Ladies and Gentlemen, we are the backbone of society! Incredulous as it sounds at this moment, it is the truth. We are the light of the world! We are His holy and chosen priesthood! We are ambassadors of Christ to the world. If we don't step up into this role, no one else will. The Church, and God Himself, will continue to be a stereotype to the world, a boneyard, and a relic of feeble mankind's need for a crutch.

One person can change the world. One person can change the world by yielding herself to the Father, receiving her identity, purpose, passion and authority from Him, her Father of Lights, and finally, by accepting His invitations, from small to great, and acting on them as He initiates. What is our role? It is to yield. He does *all* the rest.

Imagine if there were many of these "one persons," each changing the world in their own specially designed way. We would comprise an army of believers, all marching under the promptings of the Holy Spirit. How many people does it take to constitute an army? Not many; Gideon only had 300. Abram had 318. But, those were human battles. What about spiritual war? There were 120 gathered together on the day of Pentecost, awaiting the Holy Spirit. Jesus had 12. Small numbers of God's people have, in alignment with Him, changed the face of history, over and over again!

Have you received your identity from your Heavenly Father? Authority? Calling? Does He call you from sleep, just as he did with young Samuel? Do you hear His whispers during the menial tasks of the day as with Brother Lawrence?[165] Does He direct your steps each day as with Corrie ten Boom?[166] Do you converse with the Lover of your soul like Madame Guyon?[167] Do you know His still, small voice? If you cannot answer yes to these questions, then I promise you that God wants to commune with you in ways beyond your imagination.

It was perhaps summed up best by A.W. Tozer, who wrote, "Remember, we know Christ only as the Spirit enables us. How thankful we should be to discover that it is God's desire to lead every willing heart into depths and heights of divine knowledge and communion."[168]

What is the key to most everything we've examined about the Holy Spirit throughout this book? It is the emptying of self, the crucifying of our own plans and perspectives so that we can find new life in the Spirit. Can you say that you fit this description? Do you model this as the heart of Christianity? If not, what will it take for you to lay down your life so that real life can begin?

---

[165] "The Practice of the Presence of God," by Brother Lawrence and Joseph de Beaufort

[166] "Tramp for the Lord," by Corrie ten Boom

[167] "Autobiography of Madame Guyon," by Jeanne Marie Bouvier de La Motte Guyon, Thomas Taylor Allen

[168] "Whatever Happened to Worship," by A.W. Tozer

www.ingramcontent.com/pod-product-compliance
Lightning Source LLC
LaVergne TN
LVHW051559070426
835507LV00021B/2666